WATCHET REUNITED

Maurice & Joyce Chidgey

HALSGROVE

First published in Great Britain in 2008

Copyright Maurice and Joyce Chidgey © 2008

British Library Cataloguing-in-Publication Data
A CIP record for this title is available from the British Library

ISBN 978 1 84114 791 8

Halsgrove House
Ryelands Industrial Estate, Bagley Road,
Wellington, Somerset TA21 9PZ
Tel: 01823 653777
Fax: 01823 216796
email: sales@halsgrove.com
website: www.halsgrove.com

Printed in Great Britain by CPI Antony Rowe, Wiltshire

Contents

Acknowledgements

The authors are extremely appreciative of the supply of photographs, help, kindness and hospitality shown to them during the compilation of this book. Every effort has been made to be accurate using the information received, but apologise in the event of any errors or omissions.

Our sincere thanks and acknowledgements are expressed to the following for information and the loan of photographs: Virginia Nash, John Lee, Richard Walsh (*Sunday Independent)*, Mike Axon, Tony Knight, Douglas and David Parkman, Craig and Piper Norman, Steve Guscott, Roy Chave, Jack Binding, David and Daphne Milton, Knights Templar School, Nick and Julie Sully, Joyce Newsham, Michael Jones, Alison Champion, Madge Abbey, the late Raymond Clavey, the late Ben Norman, Derek Quint, Watchet Market House Museum Society, Clifford and Joyce Milton, John Coombs, Margaret Clayton, Linda Norman, Bill Strong, Alec and Bernice Danby, Arthur Langdon, Diana Tipper, Richard and Chris Burnell, Kester Webb, Keith and Joy Towells, Mollie Clinton, Sue Upstone, John Nash, Hugh and Dot Amery, Alan Woollam, Christine and Steve Waterman, Watchet Bowling Club, Ann Turley, Bristol Evening Post and Press Ltd, Somerset Studies Library, the Editor *West Somerset Free Press,* Clive Strong, Norman Yaw, Donald Butterworth, Joan Jones, Suzette Jones, Glenda Bale, Margaret Pye, Jenny Hill, Margaret Perring, Tommy Webster, Jim Martin, Dudley Binding, David Sully MBE, Tony Sully, Margaret Norman, Vernon Stone, Ken Grandfield, Watchet Cricket Club, Watchet Town Football Club, Sue Williams, John Jones, Joyce Gibbins, Elisa Day, Bob Reed, John York and Loretta Whetlor.

Thanks are also extended to Steven Pugsley and the staff at Halsgrove for their help and advice.

Maurice and Joyce Chidgey, 2008

Introduction

I t is fitting that the historic seaport town of Watchet should be the first to be featured in a new series of books by publishers Halsgrove, which incorporates in its titles the theme *Reunited*. A wide range of photographs representing people, events, groups, sport and personalities have been selected, accompanied by relevant captions and in some cases longer articles. This album-style book attempts to portray a glimpse of life in the town during the past seven decades and into the present one. It is to be hoped that the photographs will stir memories and reunite Watchet folk past and present.

In its time Watchet boasted three bakeries, a wet fish shop, three butchers, two greengrocers, three milk rounds, three full-time banks, many small corner shops, a milk bar, a thriving harbour, a large workforce at Wansbrough paper mill, a shirt factory, a paper and bag factory, three schools, a coal merchant, three garages (two with filling stations), Public Hall, two cinemas, Community Centre and a nine-hole golf course.

Watchet has a remarkable history of over 1,000 years, which includes a Saxon mint, churches, a manor house, the great storm of 1900, civic changes, commerce and industry, being a garrison town, sporting achievements, carnival (with its hard-working and enterprising club) and the transformation of the harbour into a marina. The town also boasts two prize-winning brass bands, a choral society, two museums, a uniformed town crier, a music festival and firework display, Phoenix Centre, sporting clubs and many other organisations.

Watchet is further reunited with the past with the West Somerset Railway having a station in the town. This rail link brings a considerable number of visitors, and in former years transported many local shoppers, workers and schoolchildren to Taunton, as well as goods. Playing a prominent part in attracting many visitors to this unique area, Watchet remains a fascinating town with a great community spirit.

CHAPTER 1

In the 1930s

This was a decade of many Royal occasions – firstly the Silver Jubilee of King George V in 1935 to be followed the next year by his death and the accession of Edward VIII. His reign was short-lived as he abdicated in 1936 to be succeeded by his younger brother George VI. The Silver Jubilee in 1935 and the Coronation in 1937 were celebrated with many street parties, presentation of commemorative mugs and other festivities.

The death occurred in 1933 of John Short (known locally as *Yankee Jack)*, Watchet's famous sailor and shantyman; he had reached the great age of 94.

In 1937 the west pier was split open during a terrific gale. An annual event much looked forward to was the arrival of Whitelegge's fun fair on the Esplanade for a fortnight's stay during August. Entertainment for Watchet folk was further enhanced by the opening of the Conquest Cinema in 1938.

With war clouds looming, the late 1930s saw much increased military activity at nearby Doniford, especially with the use of the Queen Bee (a radio-controlled plane) for target practice by the gunners. Like other country towns and villages, Watchet had its influx of evacuee children from London and other cities at the outbreak of war in 1939.

The advent of the Second World War, with its blackout restrictions, saw the end of an old Watchet custom, Lantern Night. It took place on 16 September and was a surviving reminder of Watchet Fair.

In the sporting world, Watchet saw one of its cricketers, Harold Gimblett, rise to fame with a sensational debut for Somerset, scoring a century in his first match in 1935. Soccer saw the Watchet club enjoy considerable success, winning many trophies. Women were invited as members of Watchet Bowling Club in 1939.

Young members of a concert party at Watchet Public Hall to celebrate the Silver Jubliee of King George V and Queen Mary, 1935. *Left to right, back row:* Ian Childs, Glanmore Rowbottom, Harold Wells; *third row:* Brandon Pryce-Jones, Sheila Langdon, Nesta Pope, Stella Binding, Monica Kemp, Valerie Hopkins, Ann Pullin, Rita Eveleigh, Mavis Chave (conductor); *second row:* Ken Langdon, Pearl McLaren, Rex Gray, Betty James, Jean Binding; *front:* Estelle Willicombe, Derek Nicholls, Norman Binding, Alan Chilcott, Eric Binding, Hilary Harris, Jill Childs, Dorothy Reed, Sylvia Perkins, Beryl Preece, Sheila Court, Muriel Chave, Desmond Hoare.

Workers at Parsonage Farm, 1930. The tenants of the farm were then Mr John Stoate together with his son Richard. *Left to right:* Tommy Paine (Snailholt Mill), Mr Lodge (farm bailiff), Bob Morle.

Mr Lodge, farm bailiff *(left)*, and Jack Starkey by the sheep dip at Parsonage Farm, 1930.

Sidney Watts, a worker at Parsonage Farm, with one of the farm's cart-horses 'dressed overall' outside 'Windwhistle' after winning first prize in the local cart-horse parade, 1930.

William Henry ('Shippy') James, 1936. 'Shippy' was a well-known local character, being employed by Watchet Urban District Council as a road sweeper; he was also town crier and street gaslamp lighter.

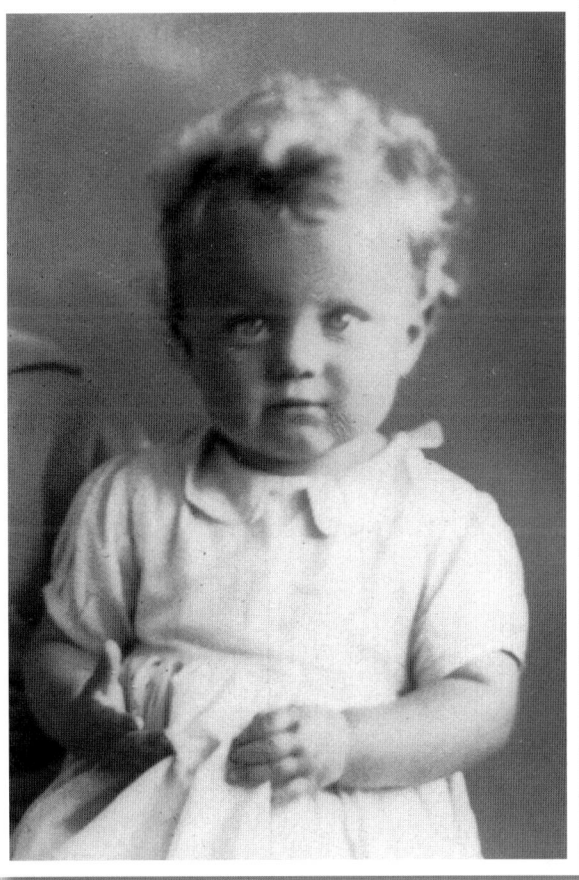

The 1935 Silver Jubilee silver commemoration cup presented to Georgina Clavey.

Georgina Mary Clavey (later Mrs Brian Kemp), eldest daughter of Mr and Mrs P.C. Clavey, was born at 6 Selgrave Terrace, Watchet, on 6 May, 1935, the Silver Jubilee day of King George V and Queen Mary. As Georgina was the only baby born that day in West Somerset, jewellers H. Samuel commissioned a silver commemoration cup, which they presented to her.

Norman and Olive
Binding in fancy
dress, 1935.

Norton's Corner, c.1938. In the 1940s/50s there were a number of small shops in the southern part of the town, including Tiley's bakery, Warren's butchers, Browning's butchers (later Mrs Norman's wool shop), Thomas' men's outfitters, Norton's grocery, McMillan's grocery, Watts' grocery, Tucker's grocery, Humphries' fish and chip shop, Co-op grocery, Canning's confectionery, Chamberlain & Jones' greengrocery, Date's grocery, etc. At the time of writing there are only two mini-markets, a cake shop/cafe, fish and chip shop and a Chinese take-away in the same area.

Watchet Town FC in unfamiliar shirts, c.1930. *Left to right:* Wally Knight, Fred Knight, Ivor Prole, Reg Hunt, Alan Pearse, Harold Gimblett, William ('Kikoe') Chorley, Walter ('Barrel') Clausen, Arthur Sully, ?, Alfred Bulpin.

Watchet Town FC, cup winners c.1937. *Left to right, back row:* Fred Chidgey, Alfred Bulpin, ?, Fred Knight, Claude Hooper, Hubert ('Cooney') Chave, ?, Alan Pearse, William Odam (holding son Raymond), Reg Hunt; *seated:* Harry Taylor, George Alexander, Fred Doble, Jack Bulpin, Wally House, Athur Sully, Fred ('Deadman') Sully, Walter ('Barrel') Clausen, Bill Clavey; *seated on the ground:* Albert ('Tiddly') Strong, Fred Strong.

Hubert ('Cooney') Chave, Watchet's
goalkeeper in the 1930's.

Watchet goalkeeper Arthur Langdon proudly
holding the Rowbarton Charity Cup, won by the
Red and Blacks during season 1939-40.

Watchet's most famous cricketer Harold Gimblett in the nets at Old Trafford, Lancashire versus Somerset, 1936. He scored 93 in the first innings and 160 not out in the second. Harold made a dream debut for Somerset against Essex at Frome in 1935 when he scored the fastest first-class century of the season in 63 minutes. Having a keen eye, his muscular shoulders and strong forearms enabled him to hit the ball with tremendous power. Harold played for England just three times and many cricket pundits thought it should have been much more. Born at Blakes Farm, Bicknoller, he died tragically in 1978 at the age of 63. A sad end to a man who had given immeasurable pleasure to cricket lovers all around the country.

CHAPTER 2
In the 1940s

In 1941 Watchet Choral Society was formed, but membership was extended to surrounding areas and is now known as the Watchet and District Choral Society.

Watchet had a platoon of the Home Guard at its formation in 1940 until it stood down in January 1945. The iron railings from the front of the Council School were among those removed for the war effort.

In 1942 a British Restaurant at the Rope Walk in South Road was built and later transformed into a Community Centre.

VE and VJ Days were celebrated in 1945 and a carnival re-started in 1946, but this only ran for a few years.

There was severe weather in the winter of 1947 with extremely heavy snowfalls which lasted several weeks. Gliddon's Foundry in Swain Street closed in 1948.

The town saw the start of considerable expansion with the building of more Council houses, including temporary prefabricated homes (prefabs) at the top of Liddymore Road.

Long Sands, c.1946. *Among those pictured are:* Eddie Chave, Terry Harris, Bob McDermaid, Trevor Stone, Cora and Shirley Perkins.

Watchet Church School's Nativity play at the Community Centre, c. 1947. *Left to right:* Ann Dell, Doreen Darter, Pearl Tucker, Philip Hurley, Joyce Stevens, Sheila Reeder, Pauline Jones, Barbara Shopland, Wendy Bulpin.

Watchet Church School present *The Queen of Hearts* at the Community Centre in the late 1940s. *Left to right:* Jenny Hunt, Nicholas Axon, Joyce Webber, Ann Lloyd, Pat Kirby; *sitting:* Daphne Pearce.

The 1st Watchet Brownie Pack, 1948. *Left to right, back:* Freda Binding, Marlene Webber, Ann Dell; *middle:* Margaret Watts, Diana McMillan, Pamela Willicombe, Dorothy Dane, Dorothy Binding, Sandra Loyns, Andrea Donaghy, Diane Jones; *front:* Ann Kirby, Geraldine Conway, Veronica Bulpin, Marceline Bulpin (Tawny Owl), Margaret Reed (Brown Owl), Elaine Morgan (Guider), Priscilla Bulpin, Merle Webber, Joy Putt.

A guard of honour formed by the 1st Watchet Brownies at the wedding of their Tawny Owl, Marceline Bulpin, and Mr Ted Peake in 1949. Brownies, *from the left:* Sandra Loyns, June Stone, Diana Baker, Merle Webber, Margaret Perring (Brown Owl), Elaine Morgan, Wendy Sully, Geraldine Conway, Janet Humphries, Marion Noble, Jackie Chave, Ann Dell. *Among the onlookers are:* Mrs Ethel Chave, Muriel Chave, Margaret Binding, Mrs Clavey.

Some members of Watchet Cricket Club on tour in South Devon, 1946. *Left to right, back row:* Jack Binding, Dennis Pugsley, Hubert Westcott, Fred Doble, Gerald Stevens, Reg Smith, Hedley Stevens (scorer), Ray Binding; *front:* Bromley Penny, Jim Bradshaw.

Watchet Cricket 1st XI, 1947. *Left to right, back row:* Jack Binding, Jim Bradshaw, Reg Smith, Dennis Merson, Mony Langdon (umpire), Alan Pearse, Charlie Martin, Dickie Ireland; *front:* Chris Milton, Bromley Penny, Jim Hurley, Arthur Ricketts.

Watchet Colts soccer squad, 1946-7. *Left to right, back row:* Brian Watts, Roy Williams, Alec Jordan, Rex Gray, Frank Webber, John Willicombe, Ernie Binding (manager); *front:* Pat Edwards, Raymond Clavey, Edgar Chapman, Donald Webber (captain), Clifford Milton, Trevor Webber, Chris Milton.

George Alexander, a stalwart Watchet footballer for many years.

Watchet Town AFC, 1945-6. *Left to right, back row:* Jimmy White, Percy Griffin, Sam Hurrell, Gerald Bellamy, Bill Tipper, Arthur Caley, Albert Chave, Hedley Stevens; *front:* Walter ('Barrel') Clausen, Fred ('Deadman') Sully, Jack Burge, Robert Binding, Alan Webber; *insets:* Les Chapman, Fred Doble, Fred Knight.

Members of Watchet ATC in the early 1940s. *Left to right, back row:* Grenville Harris, Mervyn Berryman, Brian Tucker, Ian Conway, Leslie Fuller; *middle:* Frank Kirby, Ron Prole, Derek Hawkins, Claude Binding, John Lee; *front:* Mervyn Parsons, Hector Binding, Les Stevens, Raymond ('Bunny') Binding.

Watchet Girls' Training Corps, c.1942. *Left to right:* ?, ?, Rita Bowden, Margaret Sully, Margaret Binding, Pat Willicombe, Marceline Bulpin, Florence Fisher, Delphine Morgan, Violet James, Josie Knipe.

Watchet Salvation Army Sunbeams, c.1947. *Left to right, back row:* Enid Pope, ?, Pearl Harris, Margaret Pope, Joyce Webber, ?, Jenny Webber, Ruth Norman; *middle:* Evelyn Searle, ?, ?, Christine Mozeley, Marion Jenkins; *front:* Daphne Pearce, Iris Coombs, ?.

Mrs Edwards' Dancing Class, 1949. *Left to right:* Helen Smith, ?, Ann Chamberlain, June Peppin, Sue Strong, Sue Hurley.

A group of children in Gladstone Terrace setting off for Sunday School, c.1945. *Left to right, back:* Joyce Chave, Joyce Stevens, Geoffrey Griffin, Tony Harris; *front:* Jenny Hunt, Wendy Bulpin, Dudley Binding, Robin Gardner. Peeping over her back gate is Mrs Amy Binding.

Reflections of Watchet

The authors are grateful for the following contribution by John Lee, who spent many of his boyhood and teenage years at Watchet:

I was born at Washford in 1931, the son of James (Jim) and Sarah Ellen (Nellie) Lee, and have one sister, Marion, who was born in 1930. My father was a postman with a little Postman Pat *van and was responsible for delivering and collecting mail over the Brendon Hills. I recall as a little lad sometimes getting up at 4 a.m. for the thrill of travelling around with him. We moved to Watchet around the beginning of the Second World War as my father's job was transferred to Watchet Post Office. We were allocated No. 26 South View by the Urban Council and I lived there until being called for National Service in 1950.*

I first attended Watchet Church School under the headship of Mr Earle. On qualifying for Grammar School, Mr Earle persuaded me to attend Huish's Grammar School in Taunton rather than the nearer Minehead Grammar School. This entailed a daily

journey on the 7.55 a.m. train from Watchet station, returning home at 6 p.m. There were a few other Watchet lads also going to Huish's at this time, including John Willicombe, who lived next door to us; John ('Naggers') Norman, who lived in West Street; Pat West, whose parents kept the shop next to the Post Office; and Keith ('Bunter') Manning. Travelling on the train with us, but attending Taunton School, was Moger Woolley. There may have been others, but my memory ends here.

At the same time, John, Keith and I sang in the choir at St Decuman's Church and rang the bells. Both Keith and John had excellent voices, and I remember John sang a lovely tenor after his voice broke. We attended church three times a day – morning and evening services and Sunday school in the afternoon. After Sunday school we would sometimes walk as far as Kentsford Farm and from there would return via the Mineral Line. On the way there was an orchard, but the apples were more like crab apples rather than a tasty morsel! The Vicar was a Canon Pearce, who also ran a Scout troop, to which we all belonged, but I cannot remember much about it as we were not that keen!

Our route to church took us through the fields entered near the gasworks. Keeping the fires going in the gasworks was a Mr Gunney, who also lived in South View; it was from the gasworks that we would collect coke for our fire. In charge of the gasworks was Mr Stephenson, whose daughter played the organ at church and also taught both Marion and me the piano. Marion was a better musician than I, and took some advanced certificates. She was also a member of the team who rang handbells in the church before the service on Sunday mornings as the ringing of the tower bells was not permitted during wartime only in the event of a German invasion. I was still playing the violin at this time, having started lessons whilst living at Washford, but I did not keep it up. I changed direction musically by joining the Watchet Town Band and played the cornet. The bandmaster at that time was a Mr Wedlake and sometimes we would play from the bandstand on the Esplanade; our band room was next to the Star Inn.

John and Keith left school after taking their school certificates, but I stayed on in the Sixth Form until I was called for National Service. I believe Keith joined the Post Office telephone branch, which used little green vans for transport. John took a carpentry apprenticeship, married a girl from Williton and they lived in a house in Causeway Terrace. Sadly, I heard later he had died, but well after I had left the area.

Whilst at school my main sport was football and, fortunately, this was also Huish's main winter activity. For me there was sometimes a clash on Saturdays between playing for the school or for Watchet - initially for the Casuals under Mr Chidgey and then for one of the other sides. There were occasions when, to meet both commitments, I would cycle to Taunton in the morning to play for the school and then back to Watchet to play in the afternoon. Oh to be able to do this now! Saturday evenings were usually spent in the Community Centre at dances where the usual band was either Brian Blackmore's or Brian Tucker's. The latter's parents kept a shop at the bottom of the road, near the fish and chip shop.

After National Service, rather than take a place at university, I joined the Somerset Constabulary and my first posting was at Bridgwater. I played a few soccer games for Watchet whilst there, but during that time whilst playing for the police, I sustained a serious knee injury which finished my playing days. Golf then became my main sporting activity.

I moved around the Somerset area to take up various police posts and in 1964 I moved from an inspector's post in Taunton to take command of the Minehead sub-division. This for me was a wonderful job as it covered the whole West Somerset area which I knew so well. There were magistrates' courts at Minehead, Dulverton and Williton and at that time the police did most of the prosecutions, so as sub-divisional commander this was one of my tasks. Realistically, my move to Minehead was too early in my career and in 1967 I was promoted to chief inspector and moved back to Taunton. My next promotion in January 1969 was to superintendent, when I moved to London to take up a post at the Home Office; whilst there I received a further promotion to chief superintendent.

John retired from the Police Service in 1984 and now lives with his wife Jennie at Shepton Mallet.

Watchet Harbour in the late 1940s. Note Whitelegge's fun fair on the Esplanade, which made a welcome return to the town for its annual fortnight's summer stay after absence during the Second World War years.

CHAPTER 3
In the 1950s

There were street parties and other festivities to celebrate the Festival of Britain in 1951 and the Coronation of Queen Elizabeth II in 1953. Early in the decade saw the opening of the British Van Heusen shirt factory at The Cross, Watchet (now the doctors' surgery).

The Watchet British Legion Band was formed in 1952, and 1953 saw the opening of Watchet Library at the former lifeboat station. Cliff erosion caused a section of the road at Cleeve Hill to subside onto the beach in 1954.

The 1950s saw a visit to Watchet of Wilfred Pickles with his popular radio programme, *Have a Go*, which was broadcast from a packed Community Centre.

Operating from Doniford Camp since 1945, the RAF Regiment moved to Bodmin, Cornwall, in 1956.

Watchet street names and numbers were changed in 1956, resulting in the disappearance of many old names. These included Selgrave Terrace, South View, Grove Meadows, Malvern Road, Alexandra Villas, Jubilee Terrace, Gillam Terrace, New Road, Temple Terrace, Windsor Terrace, Vale Cottages and Prospect Villas.

At the sixth annual Somerset Brass Band Festival at Crewkerne in 1956 Watchet Town Band won the C.W.L. Pinney Challenge Cup. Bandmaster T.W. Bulpin was presented with a special award and Albert Chave won a medal as the best bass drummer.

Well-known Watchet journalist and townsman Will Lee passed away at the age of 85 in 1956; he was a member of the editorial staff of the *West Somerset Free Press* for over 60 years.

In sport, Watchet Town football team won the Somerset Senior Cup in season 1955-6 and again in season 1958-9, when they were also runners-up in the League Knockout Cup.

A Causeway Street party in celebration of the Festival of Britain in 1951. *Left to right, back:* Mrs Pat Bindon (holding Paul), Mrs Pearce, Mrs N. Coombs, Mrs F. Binding, Misses Hilda and Ada Clavey, Mrs Johnson, Mrs Withers, Mrs Sully, Dorothy Reed; *around the table, clockwise from left:* Robin Pearce, Shirley Webber, Daphne Pearce, Doreen Darter (holding Ivy), Elizabeth Binding, Elizabeth Stevens, Diane Stevens, Carol and Pam Willicombe, Margaret Jones, Shirley Prole.

Aerial view of Watchet in the 1950s.

Children of Flowerdale Road and Selgrave Terrace celebrate the Festival of Britain with a party in the Church School, 1951. *Among those pictured are:* Primrose Bruford, Michael Clausen, Tony Sully, Eric Clavey, Randolph Bulpin, Doris Dane, Mrs Bulpin, Mr Bulpin, Claude Bruford, Mrs Clausen, Pat Kirby, Gladys Sully, Dorothy Dane, Mrs Jones, David Tipper, Harold

Clavey, Rosemary Bruford, Geraldine Canning, Maureen and Phillip Tipper, Janet Humphreys, Veronica Bulpin, ? Bulpin, Robert Clavey, Carol Brownsey, Diane Bulpin, Ronnie Gunney, Helen Clavey, Brian Jones, Cedric Bruford, Christine Dane, Priscilla Bulpin, Tony Clausen, Cynthia Bruford.

Causeway Terrace's Coronation party at the Council School Hall, 1953. *Left to right, back row:* Marion Watts, Nora Coombs, Dolly Stevens, Winnie Burge, Mrs Bulpin, Iris Peppin (holding Irene); *third row:* ?, Richard Binding, Lena Prole, Gwyn Saunders, Mrs Jones, Robin Pearce, Mrs Darter, John Coombs, Florrie Rowe, Elizabeth Binding, Pam Rowe, Shirley Webber, Miss Ada Clavey, Shirley Prole, ? Willicombe, Bridget Jones, Pat Oliver, ?, Mrs Webber, Mrs Johnson, Mrs Oliver, Mrs E. Binding, Myrtle Binding, Mrs Prole; *second row:* Pam Searle, Elizabeth Stevens, Dorothy Rowe, ?, Wendy Sully, ? Jones; *front:* Adrian Rowe, John Jones, Graham Watts, Douglas Edwards, Andrew Rowe, Peter and Ray Willicombe, ?, ? Jones, Rosemary Dunn.

Coronation street party at Liddymore Road, 1953. Among those pictured are Hugh Amery, Len Blackmore, Harold Binding, Anthony Short, Peter Binding, Gillian Binding, Stuart Strong, Pat Baker, Helen and Janet Amery, Mrs Betty Binding. Note the prefabricated buildings (prefabs), now demolished, which were built as temporary homes after the Second World War.

Party for West Street children at the London Inn to celebrate the Coronation in 1953. *Among those pictured are:* Steve Groves, Norman Sully, Bill Strong, Nigel Groves, Colin Norman, Jean Eveleigh, Geraldine Conway, June Bulger, Janice Webber, Christine Jones, Gillian Jones, John Stone, Keith Stevens, Marion Jenkins, June Stone, David Wilkins, Graham Wilkins, Glenys Sully, Karen Sully, Mrs Wilkins, Mrs Jenkins.

Coronation street party at Whitehall, 1953.
Among those pictured are: Blanche Diamond,
Bessie Webber, Ivy Pardoe, Jenny Webber,
Barbara Webber, John Searle, Lilian Hayhoe,
Philip Taylor, Brian Taylor.

Coronation party in 1953 for children of Grove Meadows (now Quantock Road) and adjoining streets at builder Geen
Williams' garage. *Among those pictured are:* Mrs Geen Williams, Clara Knight, Gladys Bowden, Hilda Bale, Mrs Bishop,
Elma and Helen Amery, Sue Hurley, David Allen.

Watchet's Shakespearean actress Barbara Jefford *(right)*, with her father, talking to Miss Kate Wheeler, retired schoolteacher at the Church School, on the occasion of Watchet Flower Show and Fête, 1957.

Opening night at the Watchet Home Guard Club in Goviers Lane in the early 1950s. *Left to right, back:* Major W.T. Greswell, Mr and Mrs Ivor Prole; *front:* Eric Weston, Fred Bishop, Vic Danby.

Members of the Axon family at the Coronation parade, 1953. *Left to right:* Nicholas, Lorna (Women's Section British Legion), Nolan, Michael (leader of the parade).

Ambulancemen W. Challice *(left)*, Percy Chubb and Len Binding on duty at a sporting event on the Memorial Ground in the 1950s.

A group of Watchet young ladies on the Recreation Ground, 1953. *Left to right, back:* Mo Sully, Elma Amery, Pearl Tucker, Wendy Bulpin; *front:* Jenny Hunt with Junior the dog.

Former Watchet cobbler Frank Jones with his willing 'apprentice', nephew Douglas Parkman, in the garden of Courtlands Cottages (now part of Churchill Way), c.1958. For a while Frank also had a small footwear repair workshop in High Street, Williton, which is now demolished. His father was a well-known local chimney sweep. Note the gas-holders in the background, now long dismantled.

A group of Watchet 'Likely Lads' on holiday in Jersey, 1956. *Left to right, back:* Bill Strong, Haydn Sully, David Groves; *front:* Michael Clausen, Nicholas Axon, Robin Pearce.

Watchet harbour, c.1950. The large buoys were used as markers for shipping and the small ones as targets at the Lilstock bombing range. In the harbour they were also used as diving boards by children.

The 1st Watchet Girl Guides at the Memorial Ground, 1950. *Left to right, back row:* Betty Langdon, Lorraine Prole, Marjorie Morgan, Madge Dalby, Pauline Jones, Jean Eveleigh, Jean Perring; *middle:* Joy Whittington, Christine Langdon, Shirley Webber, Elaine Morgan, Joan Perrin, Joyce Chave; *front:* Gladys James, Judy McMillan, Inez Jones, Wendy Bulpin, Jenny Hunt, Iris Coombs.

1st Watchet Girl Guides in the mid-1950s. In front is Guide Captain Betty Coggins.

Watchet Sea Scouts and Williton Scouts before embarking for Loders Camp, near Bridport, in the 1950s. *Left to right, back row:* Ken Burnett, H. Garside, Clive Hill, Malcolm Bale, David Haller; *middle:* Alan Bellamy, Chris Trebble, Trevor Morton, John Bellamy, John Branchflower, Robin Strong, Bernard Mansbridge; *among those in the front are:* Stuart McMillan, David Taylor, Tony Hemmings, Martin Bale.

Watchet Sea Scouts at camp at Sminhayes, Treborough, 1959. *Left to right:* Roger Groves, Brian Jones, Martin Bale, Alan Stephenson, David Burnell, Clive Burnell, Malcolm Bale, Richard Burnell, Jeremy Burnell, Jimmy Nicholas, Martin Downer, Richard Werren.

Paddling pool at West Street beach, c.1950.

Watchet Church School soccer team, winners of the West Somerset Schools' League, 1952-53. *Left to right, back row:* Gwyn Saunders, Roy Date, Harold Clavey, Mr. Morgan (headmaster), John Searle, Richard Binding, Richard Webber; *middle:* Tony Sully, Norman Sully, Rodney Wells; *front:* John Spence, David Jones.

Some members of the cast of a play presented by Watchet Council School at the Community Centre in 1955. *Left to right: ?,* Raymond Waterman, Bridget ?, ?, Christine Western , Doreen Attiwell, John Nicholas, Jim Nicholas, Christine Binding, Stuart Strong, Janet Amery, Peter Ross, Michael Pettifer, John Duddridge, ?, Richard Burnell, Janet Perkins, Pauline Smith, Suzanne Gunter, Philip Eveleigh, Michael Jaques.

Blessing of St Decuman's Holy Well in the 1950s. *Left to right, front:* Mr H.W. Norris and Mr A.M. Stephenson (churchwardens), Revd Alan Symon (vicar), the Bishop of Taunton and Grenville Harris.

Serving ladies for a social occasion at the Church School Hall, 1959. *Left to right:* Nora Coombs, ?, Margaret Bale, Molly Clinton, Betty Madge, Maggie-May Binding, Mrs. Sully.

Young musicians at a concert in the Community Centre, 1951. *Left to right, back:* Victor Chilcott, Eddie Chave, Kenny Moore, Jean Eveleigh, Judy McMillan, Marjorie Prosser; *front:* Brian ('Poppy') Webber.

Watchet Urban District Council, 1952-3. *Left to right, back row:* Brian Tucker, J.D. Warren, R.W. Seage; *middle:* A.L. Wedlake, W.H. West, H. McMillan, F.J. Lockyer, J. Denman, R. Werren (surveyor), J.M. Sansom (deputy clerk); *front:* H. Redd (harbourmaster), J.E. Stephens, H.S. Allen, A.E. Attiwell (chairman), F.P. Risdon (clerk), F.B. Penny, A.J. Short.

Children awaiting their Christmas presents from Santa Clause at Lodge's shop in Swain Street in the early 1950s. *Among those pictured are:* Mrs Binding, Mrs Peppin, Mrs Smith, Fred Chilcott, Keith Norman, Jenny Webber, Roy, Maureen and Janet Date, Brian Stephens, Ruth Norman, Colin Northam.

The first committee of the Watchet Sunday Night at Eight Club, 1954. *Left to right, back row:* Daphne Pearce, Iris Coombs (secretary), Molly Nicholas, Marjorie Morgan; *front:* Joyce Binding, Gill Hole, Madge Dalby.

Watchet Home Guard Club outing to commemorate the Coronation of Queen Elizabeth II, 1953. *Left to right, in the bus:* ?, ?, Priscilla Bulpin, ?, ?, Peter Bale, Rosemary Bruford, ?, Shirley Webber, Elizabeth Binding, ?, ?; *standing, back row:* Mrs Bindon, Nesta Taylor, ?, ?, Hilda Bale, Diane McMillan, Gertie Allen, Judy McMillan, Florrie Clausen, Clara Knight, Della Bulpin (holding daughter Shirley), Kathleen Bulpin (holding son Adrian), Minnie and Henry Bulpin; *front:* Brian and Philip Taylor, Stuart McMillan, Sue Hurley, Kelvin Bulpin, Diane and Veronica Bulpin.

For many years prior to the advent of the marina, mud sports took place in Watchet harbour when the tide was out. These mucky games were great fun to watch and always attracted thousands of spectators. A collection was usually made for a charity, originally for the lifeboat. Football matches and tug-of-war contests took place and these hilarious activities usually ended up with a battle royal. Some Watchet harbour mudlarkers pose for their photograph before taking part in a tug-of-war contest, c1950s. *Left to right, standing:* Gordon Allen, Jack Clavey, Eric Edwards, Ron Binding, PC Vic Newman (alias 'Dick Barton'), Victor Dalby, Steve Groves, Gordon Harris, Ben Norman; *sitting:* Bert Perkins, Bill Peppin, ?.

Watchet Town Football Club in the early 1950s. *Left to right, back row:* D. Chubb, D. Williams, J. Spoor, L. Stevens, D. Bryan, K. Bowden; *front:* A. West, B. Kemp, T. Webber, Chris Milton, A. Edwards, H. Husband.

Watchet Colts soccer squad, 1958. *Left to right, back row:* ?, Brian Stevens, Duncan Morse, ?, John Coggins, Richard Binding, Hugh Amery, Chris Groves, ?, Barry Suchley; *front:* Tony Clausen, ?, Les Allen, David Jones, Keith Stevens.

Trevor ('Cooty') Webber, a clever Watchet footballer, small in stature but large in ability.

Desmond Chubb, for many seasons a pillar of Watchet soccer team's defence.

Watchet British Legion 'A' snooker team, champions of Minehead and District Snooker League, 1950-51. *Left to right, back row:* Eric Morse, Jim Innis, Leonard Routley; *front:* Frank Webber, Sid Broomfield, Edmund Binding, Arthur Ricketts.

Dorset Horn sheep from Parsonage Farm being washed at Snailholt in the late 1950s. *Left to right:* David Burnell, Richard Burnell, Clive Burnell, Bert Coles, Tom Webber, Henry Cornish, Ernest Burnell, Bernard Calloway.

Hugh Amery holding his prize for being the winner of a sprint race at an athletics meeting at Watchet in 1956. On the left is David Groves.

The *SS Rushlight* moored at the harbourside, 1950. She brought coal from Cardiff to Watchet for Wansbrough Paper Company and was replaced by the *Arran Monarch* in 1953.

Helwell Bay in the 1950s. Note the steps down to the beach on the right, now dismantled.

CHAPTER 4

In the 1960s

The Community Centre closed and was converted into a garage and filling station in 1960. This was demolished in the 1980s and the site used for housing development. Early in the 1960s a Mothers' Club was formed in Watchet, due largely to the efforts of local nurses Virginia Nash and Pat Stowell.

The 1961 Census figures issued in 1963 showed that the population of Watchet urban district was 2,597, comprising 1,233 males and 1,364 females.

Watchet was pounded by a severe gale in January 1962, when 60-foot waves reached the top of the lighthouse. The sea tore a gap 100 feet wide in the west wall of the harbour and properties were damaged in Market Street and West Street.

There was also severe weather in 1963 with heavy snowfalls and Watchet harbour was frozen for the first time in living memory.

The eighth annual Watchet Flower Show was declared the best yet in 1963. John Tweedie was the most successful competitor in the open classes and Bill Groves in the cottagers' section.

The new Watchet Red Cross Centre on the Esplanade was opened in 1964.

Field Marshal Viscount Montgomery of Alamein was chief guest at the Vesting Day Parade for the new Royal Regiment of Fusiliers at Doniford Camp on Tuesday, 23 April, 1968.

There was a revival of trade for Watchet harbour in 1968 with the arrival of 97 ships in nine months.

Watchet harbour frozen over for the first time in living memory, 1963.

Watchet Mothers' Club concert party in the late 1960s. *Left to right:* Stella Blunt, 'Steve' Snell, Iris Champion, Betty Johns, Joyce Spoor, June Walker, Carmen Spence, Dorothy Date, Jean Howe, Josie Sheppard, ? Jacques, Nurse Pat Stowell, June Daley, Diane Coggins.

Group at Watchet Methodist Sunday School's 140th anniversary, 1964. *Among those pictured are:* Tommy Young, Jock Stronach, Revd Eric Butler, Les Amery, Revd Pennington, Arthur Pye, Mike Sheppard, Elma Hawkins, Elizabeth Pye, Margaret Pye, Lynette Burns, Linda Burke, Christine Flack, Phyllis Stronach, Betty Johns, Edna Western, Mrs Butler, Irene Pye, Christine Western, Maud Fish, Betty Penny, Ginny Nash, Mr Davis, Ivor Binding, Ian Ross, Paul Kornacki, David Howe, Gerald Sparks, Linda Downer, David Flack, Simon Chidgey, Rosemary Eveleigh, Brian Ward, Robert Chidgey, David Williams, Andrew Johns, Malcolm Boots, Brenda Ward, Suzette Blunt, Jonathan Sheppard, Christopher Sheppard, Mrs Bond, Gillian Stevens, Joy Binding, Karen Webber, Ann Redd, Valerie Smith, Hazel Baldwin, Judith Williams, Gaynor Davis, Susan Tipper, Barbara Flack, Linda Bryant, Carol Stevens, Tim Johns, Peter Williams, Carol Newbert, Julie Blunt, Julie Downer, Shelagh Davis, Glenda Bale, Joy Goostrey, Kevin Harrod.

Watchet Flower Show flower girls, 1969. *Left to right:* Valerie Smith, Julie Blunt, Christine Flack, Gillian Stephens, Judith Williams, Suzette Blunt, Rachel Whittington.

Some of the employees of the British Van Heusen shirt factory at Watchet, 1960. *Ladies sitting at the front are:* Vi Morgan, Pam Rowe, Betty Oxenbury, Jenny Webber. At this time approximately 125 people were employed at the Watchet factory.

Some of the employees of Watchet builders J.W. Date & Son on a firm's outing in the early 1960s. *Left to right:* Ben Waterman, Arthur Sadler, ?, A. Tregidgo, Brian Hayhoe, Clifford Milton, Wilf Beer, Frank Howell, Hugh Amery, Graham Chave, Alf James, Vic Vaulter, Colin Attiwell, ?, George Hayhoe, David Jones, Roy Fry.

Pleasure steamer *Balmoral* entering Watchet harbour in 1963.

Station Road (now Harbour Road) in the early 1960s, showing part of the old covered railway siding on the left. The small cottage (later used as a furniture store) adjacent to the shirt factory (now the doctors' surgery and flats) is now demolished.

A busy Watchet harbour in the 1960s. On the right is the *Kyle of Lochalsh*, a crew member of which was Watchet man Vernon Stone.

Watchet bowlers' success in winning the Mansell Cup in 1967. *Left to right:* W. Watts, E. Stone, F. Howell.

Watchet sportsman Fred Doble, who played soccer and cricket for the local teams for many years. Never at a lost for words, be was known for his dry, satirical comments on the field. During the Second World War he served with the Royal Marines and was a prisoner-of-war. Fred was also a regular contributor to the correspondence columns of the *West*

Somerset Free Press, where his caustic and witty comments on local affairs were always well read and eagerly awaited. He also contributed articles on his sporting recollections. One of the authors recollects that while playing cricket for Watchet at Tiverton many years ago Fred's dry humour came to the fore. On a hot Saturday afternoon Watchet's bowlers were being put to the sword by the Tiverton batsmen. The ball was given to Trevor Strong to have a spell with his off-spinners. Before each delivery Trevor had the habit of twisting the ball around in his hands. At the point of one of Trevor's deliveries Fred's voice could be heard from the outfield with the comment: 'Wuss got there, Trevor, a b——— clockwork mouse?' This remark brought much needed light relief to Watchet's suffering fielders, and even skipper Alan Pearse had a wry smile on his face. Fred's comment stuck with Trevor for many years.

Watchet Town FC, winners of the West Somerset Knock-out Cup in the early 1960s. *Left to right, back row:* Alfie Edwards, Jim Eslick, Des Chubb, Cliff Milton, 'Bungy' Hayhoe, Ray Odam, Ern Bale (chairman), Colin Norman, Trevor Webber, Bill Strong, Roy Fry, Harry Husband; *front:* Tony Wride, Ronnie West, Brian Redd, David Groves, David Sully.

The Ringers skittles team from the Bell Inn, 1965. *Left to right, back row:* Barry Suchley, Joe Molineux, Glyn Setterfield, Brian Goodchild , Roger Suchley; *front:* Paddy Flynn, Paul Suchley, Les Allen, Jimmy Nicholas, Chris Milton, Hugh Amery.

Watcher Council School, 1962-63. *Left to right, back row:* Mr Piper, David Howe, Stephen Williams, Stuart Norman, Malcolm Chidgey, Gordon Somerville, Mr Davies; *front:* Philip Hennig, Douglas Hayhoe, David Burnell, Stephen Webber, John Perkins, Nicholas Groves, Michael Chave.

A class at Watchet Council School, c.1963. *Left to right, back row:* Roger Norman, Stephen Borthwick, Malcolm Bindon, Brian Stiling, ?, Karl Gardner, Simon Chidgey, Mrs. P. Pugsley, ?, Alison Ross, Shelley Jones, Heather Parsons, Tracey Willicombe; *middle:* Barry Norman, Robert Hobday, Jamie Randell, Carol Robinson, Kevin Perring, Suzanne Regan, Lyn Gilchrist, ?, Debbie Willicombe, Maureen Odam, Lindsay Bishop, Marion Jones, Julie Woodley, Ann Perkins; *front:* David Tucker, Andrew Lea, Kevin Holness, Roger Lee, Gillian Willicombe, Gary Mayo, Pat Owen, Susan Jones, ?, Karen Webber, Suzanne Burns, Karen Holness, Terry Daley, Peter Bowden.

Watchet Council School choir at the West Somerset Music Festival, 1965. *Left to right, back row:* Paul Kornacki, Stephen Perkins, Robert Miller, ?, David Howe, John Routley, Susan Amies, Christine Flack, Jane Carter, Rosemary Eveleigh, Lynette Burns, Lorna Webber; *middle:* Terry Bishop, Douglas Hayhoe, Alan Knight, Andrew Bulpin, Christopher Jones, Gary Bulpin, Sheila Norman, Gillian Bennett, Hazel Baldwin, Marilyn Pugsley; *front:* Suzette Blunt, Terri Jones, Judith Williams, Ann Perkins, Karen Holness, Florence Waygood, Linda Norman, Kathleen Ross.

Watchet County Primary School hockey team, 1969-70. *Left to right, back row:* Helen Lee, Karen Bruford, Virginia Date, Barbara Sully; *front:* Julie Downer, Julie Blunt, Angela Axon, Alyson Carter.

In 1963 one of Watchet's best-known characters, Ernest Andrew Binding, retired from the Wansbrough Paper Co Ltd after 70 years of continuous service. He started work at the age of 13, working 12 hours each day, six days a week. Ernie, as he was affectionately called, was connected with the local Methodist Church all his life, being assistant Sunday school superintendent for several years. A keen soccer enthusiast, he was a referee for 17 years, an ardent Watchet Town supporter and manager of the club's Colts side in the late 1940s. He was also a member of Watchet Cricket and Bowling Clubs. Ernie died in 1967 aged 87 years.

The Bishop of Bath and Wells, Dr Henderson, led by Dudley Binding (*left*) and Nigel Swinburne at an open-air service on the Esplanade in the early 1960s.

CHAPTER 5

In the 1970s

The military departed from Doniford in 1970 after 45 years. In 1971 British Rail closed the Taunton to Minehead branch railway line, but in 1976 the line was re-opened from Minehead to Williton by the privately-owned West Somerset Railway and extended to Stogumber in 1978. A further extension to Bishops Lydeard followed the next year.

There was a considerable build up of harbour trade early in the decade. In 1977 the Phoenix machine at Wansbrough Paper Mill was opened by Princess Alexandra, but the same year also saw the closure of the Exmoor Paper and Bag Company.

With the changes in local government in 1974, Watchet lost its Urban District Council status and the Town Council was formed.

In 1976 the Watchet Society re-started the carnival. The Silver Jubilee of Queen Elizabeth II was celebrated in 1977 with many street parties and the presentation of spoons to children by the Watchet Carnival Queen.

There was a very heavy snowfall in 1978, leaving many vehicles stranded in the town with roads blocked.

For a week in the summer of 1978 Watchet was enveloped in a haze of smoke from a major fire at the wastepaper stack at Wansbrough Paper Mill. It was not only smoke that caused problems, but particles of burnt paper also filled the air and spread a considerable distance. It took fire-fighters a lengthy time to control the fire.

The Twinning Charter signing ceremony with St Renan, France, took place at Watchet in 1979, and the same year saw the opening of the Watchet Market House Museum.

Some members of the Mothers' Club entry, Henry VIII and His Six Wives, in the 1978 Watchet Carnival. *Left to right:* Liz Kerry, Elma Hawkins, Kurt Toizinger (driver), Dot Shepperd, Ann Turley, Dot Amery, Josie Hooper.

Watchet Play Group enjoying a Teddy Bears' picnic, 1979. *Among those pictured are:* 'Aunty Pat' Watson, Cath Morgan, Jenny Lake, Andrew Rendell, Paul Rogers, Andrew Ross, Catherine Stolton, Chereen Smith, Mark Sowden, Anita Stone, Robin Taylor, Wayne Thorne, Zoe Towells, Simon Upstone, Jason Williams, Beth Woollam, Paul Jones, Niall Watson, Lee Allen, Sarah Bowe, Michelle Cane, Fiona Clark, Hayley Coles, Julia Cornish, Rebecca Edwards, Michelle Eveleigh, Paul Gallagher, Victoria Harris, Suzanne Hodgson, Christopher Kerry, Cheryl Lewis, Faye Lillington, Sarah Lynch, Simon McDermaid, Timothy Meyers, Richard Pope, Leanne Powers.

The Jones girls, 1970. *Left to right:* Diane, Inez, Christine, Bridget (sister-in-law), Gillian, Pauline.

Group pictured after a tree-planting ceremony sponsored by Watchet W.I. at St Audries Court in the mid-1970s. *Among those pictured are, from the left:* Mrs Escott, Mrs Diana Bale, Mrs Eileen Woods, Mrs Axon, Malcolm Brown, Mrs Webber, Mrs Wilkins, Mr Council, Mrs Jessie Norman, Tom Milton, Mrs Gladys Milton, Mrs Peggy Wheel, Mrs Smith, Mrs Vi Knight, Mrs Grace Brown, Mrs Sylvia Newbert.

HRH Princess Alexandra receiving flowers from admiring children at the opening of the Phoenix machine at Wansbrough Paper Mill on 4 November 1977.

Watchet Conservatives' Nursery Rhymes entry in the 1978 Watchet Carnival. *Left to right, back row:* Tony Knight, Christine Mozeley; *middle:* Mary Hildick, Irene Moore, Margaret Meader, Sandra Boyd, Ethel Kirby, Joan Stevens; *front:* Sally Bellamy, Deborah Newsham, Janet Daley, Joyce Newsham, Vi Knight.

Wansbrough Paper Co.'s cricket squad, c.1970. *Left to right, back row:* Alan Hutchins, Basil Bindon, Colin Hill, Robin Hole, Basil Jones, Tony Virgin, Maurice Langdon, Stuart Norman, Mike Bishop, Ray Whittington, ? Stevens, David Chidgey, ?, Roy Chave, Mervyn Parsons, Bert Bothwick; *front:* Adrian Rowe, ?, Andrew Middlehurst, ?.

Watchet Cricket 2nd XI, 1971, *Left to right, back row:* M. Parsons (umpire), D. Chubb, Chris Milton, R. Clavey, K. Grandfield, J. Trunks, A. Hutchins, Revd. D. Thomas (umpire); *front:* T. Strong, Cliff Milton, R. Williams, D. Champion, N. Axon, D. Writer.

Watchet Cricket Team, c.1972. *Left to right, back row:* Cliff Milton (umpire), Arthur Martin, Wally Rawle, Donald Binding, David Bendle, Ron Rendell, Bill Strong, Rex Batten, Raymond Clavey (umpire); *front:* Nick Sully, Douglas Webber, Martin Spoor, Roger Suchley, Mike Jones.

Watchet cricket captain Roger Suchley *(left)* and Brian Close (Somerset captain) returning to the pavilion after tossing a coin to see who would take first knock in a Close testimonial fund match (Watchet versus a County XI) on the Memorial Ground in 1976.

Douglas Webber receiving the Watchet Cricket Club 1975 Player of the Year Cup from Clifford Milton.

Watchet Town Reserves, 1970-71. *Left to right, back row:* Mike Jones, Roger Suchley, Hugh Amery, D. Stone, Clifford Milton, Malcolm Bale; *front:* Trevor Webber, Richard Webber, Arthur Webber, Brian Stevens, Bill Strong.

Watchet Bowling Club's County Triples winners, 1973. *Left to right:* A. Mayo, J. Spoor, D. Trunks.

Victorious West Somerset Hotel skittles team, cup winners in the Watchet and District Skittles League, 1971. *Left to right:* Colin McVey, Ken Grandfield, Trevor Strong, Richard Binding, Desmond Hunt, Geoffrey Griffin, Jack Parsons, Peter and Roy Williams.

Upstarts skittles team, cup winners 1979. *Left to right,
back row:* David Bendle, Des Chubb, Ken Grandfield,
Philip Watts, Peter Williams; *front:* Hugh Amery, Roy
Williams, Roger Amery.

Proudly showing off their local catch in 1971 of a 56lb
angler fish are (*left to right*): Roy Chave, Vincent
Howells, Derek Howells.

Watchet Town Council chairman Cllr Malcolm Brown after unveiling the Watchet Explorer sign on the front of a diesel engine to mark the commencement of a train service from Minehead to Watchet run by the West Somerset Railway from April to September 1977. Ladies pictured on the platform include, *left to right:* ?, Mrs Betsy Baker, Mrs Grace Brown, Mrs Hilda Bale, Mrs Gwen Chave, ?.

Official ceremony and unveiling of the sign at Watchet to commemorate the twinning of the town with St Renan in Brittany, France, 7th April, 1979. A party of 40 from St Renan crossed the Channel to Watchet for the ceremony of the signing of the twinning charter. Among the celebrations was a lunch of traditional English fare at St Decuman's School Hall. *Left to right:* County Councillor George Wyndham, Malcolm Brown (chairman, Watchet Town Council), David Clayton (chairman, West Somerset District Council), Tom King (prospective Conservative candidate for the Bridgwater constituency), Lt-Col Walter Luttrell (Lord Lieutenant of Somerset), Mrs Luttrell, Dr Maurice De Saulle, Andre Cheminant (mayor of St Renan).

Twinning ceremony between Watchet and Saint Renan, France, 1979. *Left to right:* Lt-Col Walter Luttrell (Lord Lieutenant of Somerset), Madame Cheminant, Dr Maurice De Saulle, Monsieur Andre Cheminant (mayor of Saint Renan), Malcolm Brown (chairman of Watchet Town Council) signing the twinning charter.

Some of the children participating in the parade to celebrate the signing of the twinning charter of Watchet and St Renan, 1979. *Left to right:* Donna Binding, Lisa Chidgey, Tracey Shirlow, Sarah Norman.

Class 7 of Watchet County Primary School, 1971. *Left to right, back row:* Nick Virgin, Andrew Hall, Geoffrey Norman, Reg Hall, Robert Parsons, Richard Stone, Kevin Holness, Stuart Entwhistle, John Claxton; *third row:* Gillian Perring, Kay Sparks, Victoria Tate, Elaine Griffiths, Susan Beckworth, Carmel Watson, Alyson Carter, Lindsay Blackmore, Kim Ambrose, Helen Lee, Julie Downer, Erica Jones, ?; *second row:* Anita Bruford, Lynne Langdon, Linda Smith, Julie Munslow, Mr Robert Watt (teacher), Sandra Bryant, Jean Chilcott, Alison Thomas; *front:* ?, Paul Flynn, ?, Tim Gardner, David Crossley, Rod Ackland, Richard Borthwick.

Fancy dress competitors at St Decuman's CE Primary School fete in the mid-1970s. *Left to right, back row:* ?, Debbie Taylor, Sarah Taylor, Lynn Everett, Sarah Criddle, Rachel Charlston, Amanda Sives; *second row:* Leah Hawkins, Kaye Everett, Antony Pope, Elizabeth Bale, Sara Rew, Paula Bale, Debbie Shepperd, Joanne Chidgey, ?; *front:* Amanda and Linda Bulley, Wayne, Darren and Kevin Perkins, Geoff Redwood.

Cast of St Decuman's School Nativity play, 1975. *Left to right, back row:* Rachel Edwards, Sarah Spence, John Manley, Annette Chidgey, Sara Rew, Frank Dennett, Nicholas Groves, Debbie Shepperd; *front:* Michael Fletcher-Bryan, Nicholas Criddle, James Bran-Smith, Maxine Phillingham, Jill Binding, Michelle Noble.

Some of the participants in a St Decuman's School concert, 1977. *Left to right, back:* ?, ?, Brett Allen; *middle:* Michelle Welch, Lisa Chidgey, Susan Wells, Christine Cunliffe, Rebecca Morgan, Donna Shirlow; *front:* Lorraine Eveleigh, Donna Binding, Sarah Hole, Kerry McGee, Marie Giles.

St Decuman's School five-a-side soccer team, 1977. *Left to right:* Scott Milton, Richard Amery, Craig Walsh, Sandy Rawle, Nicholas Criddle.

Entrants from Watchet Brownies in the town's 1977 Easter bonnet competition. *Left to right:* Debra Bade, Annette Chidgey, Joanne Bee, Joanne White, Deborah Taylor, Vicki Smith, Sarah Taylor, ?, Tanya Mather, Karen Binding, Teresa Wright, Debbie Shepperd, ?.

Snow-drifts at the rear of
Gladstone Terrace in 1978.

A snow-blocked
Market Street,
1978.

The effect of a heavy snowfall on Swain Street in 1978.

A street party at Whitehall to commemorate the Silver Jubilee of Queen Elizabeth II in 1977. Whitehall came second in the competition for the best decorated street in Watchet. *Among those pictured are:* Jeanette Binding, Kevin Harrod, Lilian Harrod, Mavis Towells, Hayley Wells, Rosemary Jones, Anita Morrison, Nicola Coggins, Karen and Zoe Knox and Hayley Ross.

CHAPTER 6

In the 1980s

Heavy snowfall in 1982 resulted in Watchet being cut off by road for a few days, although a train managed to travel from Minehead as far as Williton. May 1982 saw the closure of the Van Heusen shirt factory at Watchet.

Large crowds on the East and West Piers in August 1985 witnessed the German 2800-ton vessel *Obotrita* entering the harbour. She had left Portugal bound for Watchet laden with a cargo of cork and timber.

In 1987 Watchet had a new town crier with the appointment of Alec Danby, who was provided with an appropriate uniform, and still holds this position at the time of writing.

A year of celebrations took place in 1988 to mark 1,000 years of Watchet's history, which included a party of visitors and dancers from Denmark, home of the Vikings who invaded Watchet in 988.

A new headquarters for Guides and Brownies was opened at Watchet in 1980.

The demolition of Watchet's two gas-holders (top of South Road) took place in 1988.

The Watchet County Primary School in South Road was closed in the late 1980s and pupils transferred across the road to St Decuman's School.

Michael Sully receiving the key from Brownie Stacey Lillington to officially open the new headquarters of Watchet Brownies and Guides in 1980. Other Brownies and Guides, *left to right:* Samantha Lawrence. Sarah Criddle, Anne Le Poidevin, Elizabeth Bale, Annette Chidgey, Sharon Pope, Jane Bendle.

Watchet Cricket XI in the 1980s. *Left to right, back row:* Mervyn Parsons (umpire), Wally Rawle, Nick Sully, Steve Bryant, Mike Jones, Donald Binding, David Taylor (umpire); *front:* Edward Martin, Ron Rendell, Paul Date, Adrian Griffiths, Martin Strong, Andy Milton.

Clive Strong receiving Watchet Cricket Club's Player of the Year award from Somerset cricketer Colin Dredge in 1987. In the centre is former Watchet player Clifford Milton.

Watchet's 'Jackdaws' perched on the rail at the Memorial Ground in the 1980s!! *Left to right:* Roy Williams, Des Chubb, John Perkins, Clifford Milton, Rex Batten.

Members of the Wansbrough Paper Mill team who played Taplow Paper Mill in a sponsored cricket match in 1988. The match was organised by Jim Martin from Wansbrough Paper Mill and £535.34 was raised for the Leukaemia Research Fund. *Left to right, back row:* Clifford Milton (umpire), Steve Moore, Andy Milton, Clive Strong, Dave Dobson, Mark Clausen, Andy Trunks, Raymond Clavey (umpire); *front:* Graham Perkins, Scott Milton, Jim Martin, John Buckingham, David Knight.

The Mishaps ladies' skittles team from the Anchor Inn in the 1980s. *Left to right, back row:* Eve Goostrey, Pauline Rigby, Richard Williams (sticker-up), Mandy Power, Joy Towells; *front:* Ellie Groves, Christine (Mozeley) Somerfield, Janet Stevens.

The Ringers ladies' skittles team who played at the Bell Inn, 1981. *Left to right, back row:* Alf Nolan (sticker-up), Lilian Harrod, Dot Amery, Rose Jones, Brenda Webber, Denise Binding; *front:* Jean Wilson, Shirley Binding, Gina Cotton.

Players who participated in a 24-hour darts marathon at the Anchor Inn in 1989 to raise money for Leukaemia Research. *Left to right, back row:* Bill Pugsley, Jim Martin (organiser), Graham Evans, Wendy Martin, Cliff Evans, Kelvin Mayne; *front:* Brian Winter, Colin Midwood, Robert Yaw, Dave Pope. During 1989 a total of £505.50 was raised for the Leukaemia Research Fund through events held in Watchet organised by Jim Martin.

Organisers of a duck race at Watchet in aid of cystic fibrosis in 1988. *Left to right:* Town Crier Alec Danby, Melanie Woollam, Graham Coggins, Sheila Clavey.

Mrs Saunders' Class at St Decuman's School, 1988. *Left to right, back row:* Susan Webb, Natalie Potter, Katie Knight, Felicity Bulpin, Laura White, Sophie Routley, Victoria Chave; *third row:* Matthew Stevens, Michael Corlett, Gavin Duenas, Adrian Chick, Matthew Cox, Ross Appleby, Ian Barrass, Laura Ketchen; *second row:* Mr Alan Woollam (head teacher), Claire Cridge, Sean Kenny, Matthew Naum, Steven Smith, Hilary Dalwood, Emma Harris, Carla Martin, Siobhan Gallagher, Mrs Anne-Marie Saunders (teacher); *front:* Becky Bulpin, Gillian Bissell, Wendy Hudson, Marie Hudson, Sally Hudson, Elizabeth Turner, Peter Harding.

Mrs Collinson's Class at St Decuman's School, 1989. *Left to right, back row:* Stuart Cowling, Edward Hudson, Victoria Moore, Sarah Gibbons, Ben Edwards, Clare Rendell; *third:* Hayley Stafford, Jo Chidgey, Andrew Wide, Amy Naum, Carla Jackson, Jonathan Aldridge, Lydia Barnes, Emma Jones; *second:* Mrs Sue Upstone, Luke ?, Tammy Sowden, Angela Dalwood, Daniel Thorne, Mrs. Mavis Collinson, Henry Bissell, Alison Webb, Sarah Milton, Susannah Rogers, Mrs Jeanette Bowden; *front:* Terri Daley, Mercedes Robinson, Cheryl Dennis, Michelle Barker, Katie Bulpin, Stacey Willicombe, Ross Owen, Mark Norman.

Presentation of commemorative shields to Walter Bulpin *(left)* and Fred Bishop (bandmaster) by Roy Chave (chairman of Watchet Town Council) to mark their long service to Watchet Town Band, 1982.

Prizewinners at the Watchet Easter bonnet parade, 1982. *Left to right:* Melanie Lewis, Lisa Chidgey, Karen Amery.

Watchet Mothers' Club 25th anniversary dinner, 1986. *Left to right, back row:* Jo Willicombe, Pam Thomas, Josie Hooper, Sheila Williams, Betty Williams, Betty Setterfield, Anne Reeder, June Phillingham, Jane Don, Daphne Woods, Pat Phillips, Daphne Milton, Sheila Webb, Ann Turley, Diane Coggins, Winnie Date, Jean Howe, Valerie Webber, Valerie Norman; *front:* Joyce Spoor, June Daley, Iris Champion, Josie Sheppard, Stella Alexander, Marjorie Peppin.

Watchet harbour's east wharf in the 1980s.

Winter around Watchet in the 1980s.

Dismantling the 80ft. gas-holder at South Road, Watchet, 1985.

The voyaging theatre ship *Fitzcarraldo* visiting Watchet in 1988 when performances of *Walk the Plank* were staged on her.

Tommy Perkins leading the Watchet Carnival parade in 1982.

Watchet Carnival personalities, 1981. *Left to right, back:* Mrs F. McGinley (carnival glamorous grannie), Kim Harris and Annette Pope (carnival queen attendants), Jennifer Cordell (carnival princess); *front:* Alison Date (carnvial queen).

Watchet Mothers' Club entry The Garden Party in the town's Carnival, 1983. *Left to right, back:* Jane Don, Betty Webber, Josie Sheppard, Margaret Pope; *front:* Anne Reeder, Ann Turley.

The 1st Watchet Brownies' entry of Liquorice Allsorts in the 1981 Watchet Carnival. *Left to right, back row:* Karen Knox, Sara Rew, Liz Hamshere, Bernice Danby (Tawny Owl), Margaret Pye (Brown Owl), Maryon White; *middle:* Nicola Clausen, Chantelle Binding, Susan Wells, Jayne Newbold, Lisa Chidgey, Stacey Lillington, Laura Webber, Karen Amery, Samantha Lawrence; *front:* Sian Walker, Samantha Woodberry, Teresa Giles, Corrie Smith, Alison Pope, Siobhan Gallagher, Hayley Wells, Tara Kenny, Nicola Reed, Angela Smith, Lorraine Curtler.

The Odds and Ends, who won first prize for their Down Mexico Way entry in the 1982 Watchet Carnival. *Left to right, back row:* Ivy Darter, Eileen Nicholls, Doreen Coleman, Sheila Williams, Molly Willicombe, Elizabeth ('Bish') Boots, Joan Boots; *middle:* Joyce Chidgey, Pat Binding, Joyce Spoor, June Phillingham, Iris Champion; *front:* George and Fred Boots.

Alison Pope being crowned 1987 Watchet Carnival Queen by the previous year's Queen, Mandy Perkins.

Caroline Spence making her Brownie Promise at her enrolment to the 1st Watchet Brownie Pack in 1983. Also pictured are Brown Owl Margaret Pye (*left*) and Tawny Owl Bernice Danby.

1st Watchet Brownies Cheryl Lewis (*left*) and Faye Lillington meet Princess Anne at a 'Save the Children' reception at Dunster Castle, 1985. Standing behind the Brownies is Tawny Owl Bernice Danby.

2nd Watchet Brownies, 1988. *Left to right, back row:* Victoria De Portela e Prado, Sheena Neyens, Helen Stainton, Kirsty Martin, Michelle O'Leary, Claire Cridge, Catherine Gibbons, Danielle Norton, Michelle Nicholas; *middle:* Briony Norton, ?, Hilary Dalwood, Gillian Bissell, Anna Barnes, Sian Walker, Emma Wilder; *front:* Natalie Potter, Dawn Webber, Lorraine Mather, Helen Cridge.

A group of Watchet Brownies after experiencing a night's camping at a Guide camp in the grounds of Fairfield House, Stogursey, 1989. *Left to right:* Hilary Dalwood, Dannielle Norton, Helen Sainton, Victoria De Portela e Prado, Michelle O'Leary, Lorraine Mather. In the background is Tawny Owl Bernice Danby.

Watchet Guides and Brownies, 1980. *Left to right, back row:* Mandy Cooper, Debbie Rouse, Kimberley Cooper, Sara Rew, Annette Chidgey, Suzanne Cooper; *third row:* Debbie Taylor, Joanne Bee, Sarah Taylor, Kay Everett, Ruth Le Sadd, Elisa Chave, Lisa Chidgey, Anne Le Poidevin, Debbie Shepperd, Greshna Baxter; *second row:* Dawn Yard, Rebecca Chidgey, Bernadette Griffin, Marie Giles, Audrey Manning, Caroline Brooks, Samantha Lawrence, Ruth Edwards, Stacey Lillington; *front:* Zoe Watson, Emma Reed, Chantelle Binding, Heather Manning, Samantha Burge, Natasha Crump, Julie Gould, Sandra Williams, Samantha Searle.

Proudly holding her Queen's Guide certificate in 1982 is Watchet Guide Helen Barnett, who was also presented with a Queen's Guide badge. Also pictured are, *left to right:* Karen Yard, Anne Le Poidevin, Ruth Edwards, Dawn Yard, Annette Chidgey, Sarah Criddle, who were the recipients of various other Guide badges.

The Robins Patrol of the 1st Watchet Girl Guides being presented with the Anson Trophy in the grounds of Dunster Castle at the St George's Day parade, 1988. *Left to right:* Edith Webb (Somerset County Commissioner), Katrina Stickley, Zoe Towells, Leanne Power, Sarah Doble, Helen Ayres, Angelina Norton.

Group of Watchet ladies on a sponsored walk in 1981 to raise funds in aid of a scanner for a Bristol hospital to help local lad Kevin Perring. *Left to right, back:* Jackie Kane, Wendy Mainwaring, Mandy Curtis, Dorothy Amery, Joyce Milton, Brenda Webber, Margaret Welch; *front:* Margaret Perring, Valerie Mainwaring.

Watchet Town Council, 1982. *Left to right, back row:* Alec Danby, Tony Knight, Nigel Cotton, Major Alex Gordon MBE, Malcolm Brown, Bob Perrett (clerk); *front:* Doris Barron, Joyce Flack, Jean Howe, Roy Chave (chairman), Ethel Kirby, Eileen Woods MBE.

In July 1987 one of Watchet's best known personalities, Bromley Penny, celebrated his 90th birthday. Mr Penny – known to everyone as Brom – was a retired businessman and cricket enthusiast, former Sunday school superintendent and one of the longest serving stewards in the Methodist Connexion. To honour the occasion Brom, accompanied by his wife Betty, was entertained in the Methodist Church Schoolroom, where he was presented with a commemorative carving, 'Praying Hands', by the church's senior steward Jack Binding. *Left to right:* Alec Danby (town crier), Bromley Penny, Betty Penny, Jack Binding.

Some of the group of Danish dancers who visited the town in 1988 to join in the Watchet 1,000 celebrations.

In the 1990s

St Decuman's School was closed and the new Knights Templar CE and Methodist Community VA School opened in 1990. Watchet ceased to be a working port and the harbour deteriorated, but later in the decade plans were discussed for the building of a marina.

Heavy seas and gale force winds caused considerable damage to the town and coastal area in February 1990. A baby girl was plucked to safety when huge waves crashed into her bedroom at Beach Cottage, West Street, at the height of the gales. In 1991 the Baptist Church at Little Causeway was closed and relocated at the former St Decuman's School.

The Watchet branch of the National Westminster Bank closed in 1992. Watchet 1st XI was Division One champions of the Somerset Cricket League in 1992.

In 1993 Watchet Town Band reached its centenary and the same year saw the opening and dedication of Watchet Cemetery. The 50th anniversaries of VE and VJ Days were marked in the town with parades and other festivities in 1995.

A Viking Festival was held in 1998 with the re-enactment of a Viking invasion.

Last day of the Watchet branch of the National Westminster Bank branch in Swain Street, 27th November 1992. *Left to right:* Jill Manuel, Joy Towells, Michael Dodd (manager), Tristan Scott, Roy Bulpin, Alison Bashford.

Last group photograph of St Decuman's School before moving to Knights Templar in 1990. Headmaster Alan Woollam is in the centre. The old building was demolished in 2007 and the site developed into a housing complex named Woollams Place after the old school's last head.

Staff and church representatives of Knights Templar VA First School, 1992. *Left to right, back row:* Sue Wood, Mavis Collinson, Shirley Moore, Brenda Gallagher, Adrian Regis, Pat Binding, Gill Naum, Dawn Plumbley, Liz Foster; *third row:* Val Kenny, Jackie Heywood, Jenny Owen, Anne-Marie Saunders, Judy Carslake, Doreen Broom, Lyn Martin, Glenda Bale, Daphne Milton; *second row:* Kathleen Morgan, Rachel Binding, Edna Buckley, Audrey Chapman, Brenda Wilson, Marion Pyne, Jean Burge, Margaret Perring, Sarah Wetherick, Georgie Badcock, Pauline Bennett; *front row:* Karen Wedlake, Sandra Mead, Preb Michael Barnett (Vicar of St Decuman's), Alan Woollam (head), Barbara Stainton, Revd Gordon Elford (Methodist minister), Pat Woolgrove.

Knights Templar First School football teams, 1995. *Left to right, back row:* Sam Tapp, Ross Bishop, Joe Duenas, Damelle De Portela e Prado, Stephen Waygood, Michael Taylor, Martin Chappell, Simon Potter; *middle:* Jack Munro, Jason Gitsham, Daniel Cawthorn, Sam Tame, Trevor Williams, Sam Wood, Ben Lobley; *front:* Andrew Seyforth, Daniel Mossman, Ian Trunks, Lee Knowles, Daniel Allen, Billy Banks, Alex Appelby.

Girls' Catchball squad at Knights Templar First School, 1995. *Left to right, back row:* Emma Needs, Kelly Allen, Charlotte Hudson, Elizabeth Stevens, Stacey Blackmore; *middle:* Jessica Binding, Alice Stanbury, Nicola Dobson, Danielle De Portela e Prado, Emma Power, Emma Sully, Sian Jones; *front:* Emily Turner, Samantha Blair, Laura Bryant, Nicola St John, Catherine Overall, Holly Sowden, Rebecca Clark.

A 'wedding' group at Knights Templar First School, 1995. *Left to right*: Jason Strong, Jodie-May Cook, Sarah Trunks, Jason Smith, Jamie Milton.

'All aboard the Watchet Red Cross Special', celebrating the centenary of the Red Cross in 1995. *Left to right:* 'Taff' Morgan, Jean Howe, Eileen Tapp, Malcolm Brown, Peter Darrell, Elizabeth Phillips, Ruth Blackmore, Ginny Nash, Town Crier Alec Danby, Joan Bosley Ann Lewis, Diana Bale, Muriel Taylor.

A party from the Watchet Red Cross Centre visited Italy in 1997. Their destination was Solferino, the battlefield, which, being witnessed by Henri Dunant, subsequently led to the founding of today's Red Cross and Red Crescent movements. Pictured visiting the museum near Solferino are: *clockwise from left:* Jean Howe (front, holding papers), Mavis Bryant, Faye Ross, Jessie Norman, Grace Brown, Liz Hampshere, Joan Bunyan, Peter Pope, Malcolm Brown, Kit Hammond, Anne Wright, Robert Wright, Yvonne Swinburne, Peggy Waterman, Nigel Swinburne, Joyce Hedge, Rodney Ettery, Margaret Morgan, Sid Lloyd, Edwin May, Gwen Ettery, John Taylor, Joy Towells, Keith Towells, Dennis Pugsley, Phyllis Pugsley, Muriel Taylor, Eileen Tapp, Brenda Pope, Donald Tapp, Edith Reynolds, Christopher Reynolds, Ann Lewis, Joan Bosley.

Presentation of hygiene certificates to members of the Watchet Red Cross, 1999. *Left to right:* Bernice Danby, Ruth Lynch, Cynthia Hulme, Janet Waterman, Daphne Barrass, Edna Adams, Margaret Morgan.

A drilling rig pictured outside Watchet harbour in the late 1990s.

The centre of the picture shows the chimney stack (demolished in the 1990s) at the old Stoate's flour mill (later Exmoor Paper and Bag factory which closed in 1977). The building was re-occupied in 1978 by Watchet Products, who remained there for 30 years until relocating to Upcott Farm Industrial Units, Bicknoller, in 2008. At the time of writing, the site of the old flour mill has been ear-marked for the building of an elderly persons' care home.

Retirement of Watchet postman Alec Dandy, 1993. *Left to right:* Martin White, Richard Gill (obscured), Steve Thompson, David Fry (town crier of Kingswood, Bristol), Michael ('Zippy') Shopland, Charles Lynch, Bernice Danby, Alec Dandy, Jeff Rogers, Philip Taylor (sub-postmaster), Mike Martin, ?, Jenny Taylor, Jenny Lake, Dot Amery with dog Oscar.

Recipients of 25 years long service awards at Wansbrough Paper Mill, 1993. *Left to right, back row:* Steve Waterman, Michael Gould, Steve Giles; *middle:* Bill Laramy, Bob Sadler, Roland Lewis, Stuart Norman, Kelvin Elsworthy; *front:* Clifford Tarr, Ron Perkins, Jimmy Lindsey, Basil Jones, Ernest Adams.

Toasting Watchet's success in being one of only six national winners of £1million each in a rural challenge run by the Rural Development Commission in 1994. *Left to right:* ?, Fay Ross (local County Councillor), Lord Shuttleworth (Rural Development Commission), Megan Lyons (Chair, West Somerset District Council), Nigel Edwards (Watchet member, West Somerset District Council), Alec Danby (Watchet town crier), Humphry Temperley (Chair, Somerset County Council), ?, Colin Rockall (Chief Executive, West Somerset District Council), Tony Knight (Watchet Town Councillor/Regeneration Partnership), Winifred Curran (Watchet Town Councillor).

Watchet Home Carers, 1996. *Left to right, back row:* Donna Chilcott, Edward Bloyce, Marlene Gulliford, Sonia Alexander (Warden, St Audries Court), ?, Sylvia Hole, Valerie Nicholls; *front:* Pam Clavey, Joyce Milton, Ann Chamberlain, Bridget Jones, Christine Bendle.

In 1990 the 2nd Watchet Brownies marked the retirement of Brown Owl Bernice Danby with a farewell presentation. *Left to right, back row:* Christine Chave, Katie Barnes, Lisa Chidgey (Snowy Owl), Emma Jones, Lisa Milton, Joanna Stickley (Young Leader), Annette Dickinson (Tawny Owl); *middle:* Victoria Moore, Alexandra Hughes, Vicky ?, Bernice Danby, Catherine Gibbons, Gillian Bissell, Rebecca Wright, Carla Wilkinson, Kimberley De Portela e Prado, Lydia Barnes, Elizabeth Pyne; *front:* Sarah-Jane Wood, Clare Rendell, Susannah Rogers, Angela Smith, Sarah Gibbons, Sinead Long.

In 1990 Watchet 2nd Brownies enjoyed a week's pack holiday at Wells and were taken on many excursions. *Left to right, back row:* Annette Dickinson (Tawny Owl), Sian Walker, Helen Cridge, Lorraine Mather, Victoria De Portela e Prado, Michelle O'Leary, Helen Stainton, Joanna Stickley (Young Leader), Sarah Criddle (Snowy Owl); *kneeling:* Rebecca O'Leary, Victoria Wood, Lydia Barnes, Lisa Milton, Katie Barnes, Sarah-Jane Wood, Hilary Dalwood, Rebecca Wright, Carla Wilkinson.

2nd Watchet Brownies, winners at the Brownie Swimming Gala, 1993. *Left to right, back row:* Lisa Milton, Catherine Gibbons, Emma Jones, Rebecca Wright, Lindsay Webber; *front:* Sinead Long, Kimberley De Portela e Prado, Sarah Gibbons, Tanya Williams.

The 1st Watchet Brownie Pack, 1995. *Left to right, back row:* ? Cole, Jessica Binding, Nicola St John, Margaret Pye (Brown Owl), Joanne Ford, Emma Sully; *middle:* Jemima Baker, Emma Turner, Stacey Blackmore, Harriet Saunders, Lauren Wilkinson, Rachel Milton, Emma Champion, Kate White; *front:* Christy Holness, Leanne Arthington, Jenny Mossman, Kayleigh Thorne, Polly Needs.

Tripping the light fantastic at the Brownie and Guide Show at Watchet Methodist Church Hall in the early 1990s. *Left to right:* Moira Manley, Margaret Pye, Liz Hamshere, Bernice Danby, Sara Rew, Maryon White.

Watchet Youth Club event winners, 1990. *Left to right:* Peter Tapp, Marie Turner, Dean Jones, Kevin Coveney, Matthew Jones, Sallie Collinson, Alan Reynolds.

Fred Knight was born on 29 December 1909, being the ninth of the ten children of William and Selina Knight, of West Street, Watchet. His sisters and brothers were Rose (Stevens), Ada (Prole), Fredrick William, Eva (Woodbury), Edwina (Bulpin), Hilda (Bale), Wallace, Vera (Wilkins) and Phyllis (Edwards/Spoor). Educated at Watchet Council School, Fred's first employment followed in his father's footsteps with the railway. In 1926, at the age of 17, he joined the packing department of the Wansbrough Paper Mill where, apart from service with the Armed Forces, he remained until retirement in 1974. He became foreman of the finishing department and was held in high esteem by both management and workmates.

On Boxing Day, 1939, Fred married Violet Parsons at the Church of St Michael the Archangel, Alcombe, and they subsequently spent all their married life at Watchet, firstly in Anchor Street, then Claremont (now Almyr House), before moving to the newly-built Woodland Road after the Second World War. They had two sons, Tony and David, who carry on the family tradition of being active within the community – Tony with his council and other work and David in the field of sport.

During the Second World War Fred served in Egypt and Italy with the Eighth Army Pioneer Corps, and as company sergeant major he was twice mentioned in Despatches for distinguished service. He wrote down his thoughts at the time and a most poignant section reads: *Next we advanced to Jerqusla to take over duties of guards on a vehicle park. It was at this depot I had my first narrow escape, being fired upon by a lone Jerry raider. God alone knows how I came through to tell the tale; four men were killed in this surprise raid. (I thank God for being merciful to me.)*

Fred's passion for soccer was something of a legend and his playing years for Watchet spanned almost three decades. His involvement with the Watchet club as committee member, assistant treasurer and team treasurer continued well into his 80s, and he later became president, a post he held until the end of his life on 28 June 1998. Together with Vi he worked to raise funds for the building of Watchet Football Clubhouse, and they continued for many years helping to run weekly bingo sessions. Both were true workers for the community and much sympathy was expressed over Vi's tragic death following a road accident in 1984.

Besides serving on the War Memorial Ground Management Committee, Fred was also a member of St Decuman's Church where he had been a choirboy and, following retirement, a sidesman. His great love of gardening saw him working on allotments in West Street (now Greenway) and at church fields along the railway bank (now totally overgrown). Through the church stewardship scheme under the Revd David Jones he looked after gardens for the elderly.

Fred was a founder-member of the Italy Star Association. He was an enthusiastic supporter of Watchet Town Band, to which many members of his family, including his brother Bill and brother-in-law Tom Bulpin, belonged. He also enjoyed travelling with the band to Hammersmith in the 1960s to support them in national competitions. At the time of writing, his nephew, David Wilkins, is a leading member of the band. When the local bands played in the streets around the town, especially at Christmas, Tony recalls that although you gave money to both, it was always that little extra for the Town Band!

A true man of Watchet, Fred has left the legacy of his sons and grandchildren, Kirsty, Katie, Callum and Warren, as they too play their part in the town he so loved.

Watchet Amateur Boxing Club, 1991. *Left to right, standing:* ?, David Ackland, Liam Gallagher, David Steele, ?, ?, Mark Cane, Russell Cowling, Andrew Christian, Danny McGee, Richard Cross, Clive Goodrum; *front:* Beresford Manley, Paul Raymond, Geoffrey Cross, Ben Collinson.

Watchet Royal British Legion 'A' with trophies won in the Minehead and District Snooker League during the season 1993-4. *Left to right, back:* Robert Yaw, Colin Milton, Norman Yaw; *sitting:* Steve Waterman, Nick Virgin. In the 1990s the team had considerable success in the Minehead and District Snooker League, winning the Division One Championship and the Open and Division One Knockout Cups several times. At the age of 14, Norman Yaw became the youngest champion of the Minehead and District Snooker League and has gone on to win the title a further eight times; he and his brother Robert have been doubles champions 12 times. Norman has also won the Merit Table many times and represented Somerset, Wessex and the League.

Geoff Rowe about to present Robert Yaw, of Watchet Royal British Legion 'A' snooker team, with a plaque to commemorate his achievement in 1993 of being the first player to record a 100 break in the Minehead and District Billiards and Snooker League.

Watchet Bowling Club's County Pairs finalists, 1999: Bill Strong *(left)* and Simon Bruford.

Watchet Cricket Club skittles team, c.1990. *Left to right, back row:* Andrew Norman, Andy Milton, Mark Milton, Stuart Cowling (sticker-up); *front:* Norman Yaw, Richard Milton, Nick Virgin.

Andy Pyne *(left)* and Michael Stout, pairs winners in the Watchet and District Skittles League, 1990.

Watchet Ladies' Foreign Legion skittles team, winners of the *West Somerset Free Press* Shield, 1991. *Left to right, back row:* Joyce Owen, Wayne Thorne (sticker-up), Sandra Holness, Ellie Groves; *front:* Chris Allen, Bridget Jones, Diane Allen.

Anchor 'B' skittles team, 1997. *Left to right, back:* Colin Norman, Nick Tapp; *middle:* Siobhan Gallagher, Keith Strong, Raymond Odam, John Jones, Roy Chave, Nick Sadler; *front:* Hugh Amery, Brian Stevens, Cedric Lewis.

Watchet Town 1st XI in the early 1990s. *Left to right, back row:* David Knight, Piers Jones, Kevin Holness, Nick Criddle, Dick Furse, Andy Hill, Bob Arthington, Nick Sully, Norman Yaw; *front:* John Wilkinson, Noel Munson, Fraser Adams, Steve Moore, Robbie Roberts, Mark Clausen.

Watchet FC Under 13s, 1997. *Left to right, back row:* Adam Moore, Andy Moore, Andrew Hutchinson, Wayne Merrick, Ben Saddington, Craig Owen, Jamie Munro, David Milton; *front:* Liam Groves, Nick Jones, Joshua Moore, Phillip Milton, Andrew Baker, Jack White, Myles Jones, Dean Stafford.

Watchet Cricket Club 1st XI, 1992. *Left to right, back row:* Philip Sylvester, Sandy Rawle, Nick Criddle, Andy Milton, Scott Milton, Mark Rawle; *front:* Andrew Norman, Clive Strong, Martin Strong, Robert Yaw, Richard Milton.

Watchet Cricket Club trophy winners, 1994. *Left to right:* Steve Perkins, Scott Milton, Clive Strong, Nick Virgin.

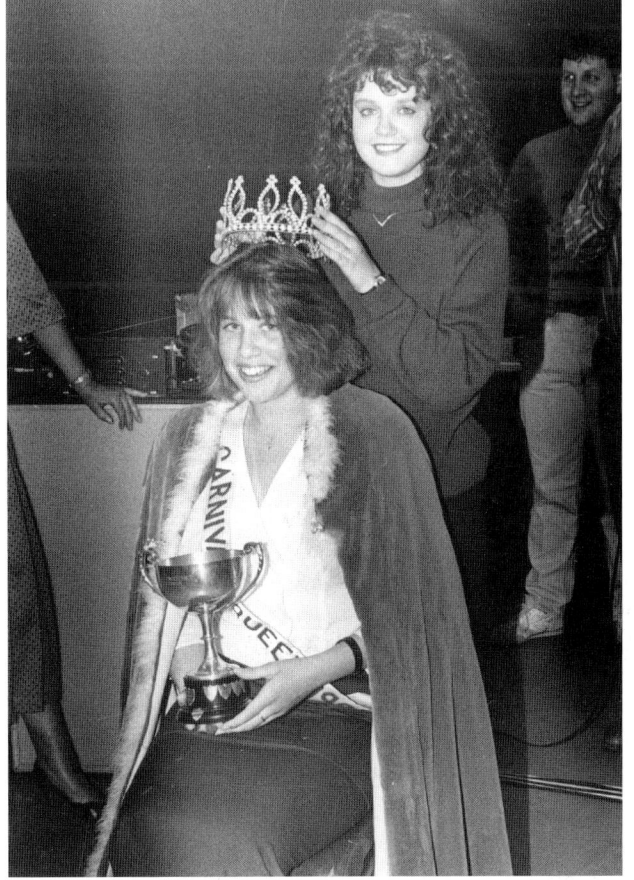

Tara Kenny crowns her successor Emma Chave as Watchet Carnival Queen, 1991.

Emma Chave (previous year's Queen) crowns her sister Sally as 1992 Watchet Carnival Queen. *On the left* is Gail Sinclair.

1st Watchet Beaver Scouts' Smugglers entry in Watchet Carnival, 1992. *Among those pictured are:* Mary Cox, Aaron Wilkinson, Billy Banks, Simon Tew, Stephen Waygood, Craig Owen, David Milton, Nick Jones, Adam Moore, Jack White, Richard Bruford, Ben Hewson, Phillip Milton, Rachel Binding, Callam Edwards, Ben Waterman, Martin Ketchen.

Watchet Mothers' Club with their entry of Les Pierrots in the 1993 town carnival. *Left to right:* Ann Turley, Joan Ridley, June Daley, Josie Sheppard, Stella Alexander, Kay Knight, Pam Thomas, Jane Don, Alison Pope, Daphne Milton, Pam Pope, Samantha Lawrence, Suzette Jones.

Watchet Carnival Queen Victoria Chave surrounded by Town Criers (*left to right*) Trevor Hekks (Trowbridge), George Carpenter (Wootton-under-Edge) and Tony Evans (Nailsworth), 1994. It was a unique occasion for Victoria as she was the third Chave sister to be crowned Watchet Carnival Queen, emulating Emma and Sally.

Well-known Watchet personality Tommy Webster, No.1 Wurzel in the Anchor Inn's float Arkwright's Ho-Down entered in the 1996 Watchet Carnival.

Members of the Anchor Inn's entry of Arkwright's Ho-Down in the 1996 Watchet Carnival. *Left to right, back row:* Pam Perkins, Tommy Webster, Debbie Russell, Siobhan Gallagher, Denise ('Flower') Ross, Paula Milton, Steve ('Trigger') Elgar; *middle:* Cindy Russell, Pauline Puttock; *front:* George Russell, Tom Creed.

The 1996 Watchet Carnival Queen and her Princesses. *Left to right, back:* Lisa Gambin, Jo Lenton, Laura Whittal; *front:* Holly Pietrasz, Kimberley Gambin.

Members of the Watchet Red Cross winning float Celebrating 80 years of Medical Loan in the 1998 Watchet Carnival. *Left to right:* Bernice Danby, Sam Mason (TV presenter, carnival guest of honour), Muriel Taylor, Jean Howe, Edwin May, Jessie Norman, Eileen Tapp, Donald Tapp.

Members of the Blues Carnival Club, winners of their class, best float and best overall entry in the 1998 Watchet Carnival with their entry of Souvenirs in Watchet Blue. *Left to right, back row:* Ethel Kirby, Diane Albutt, Jo Willicombe, Emma Sully, Iris Champion, Jenny Hill, Tony Knight, Davina Le Rendu (Carnival Queen), Kirsty Knight, Philip Jarman; *front:* Matthew Tickner (driver), June Roberts, Sam Mason (TV presenter, who presented the awards), Joyce Chidgey.

Watchet Town Crier Alec Danby, 1990 Champion of the Ancient and Honourable Guild of Town Criers.

Nursing experiences at Watchet

Sister (more usually known as Nurse) Virginia Nash relates some of her experiences since coming to Watchet in September 1957. She completed general nurse training at St Peter's Hospital, Chertsey (St Thomas' wartime hospital), and midwifery at Queen Charlotte's Hospital, London, and Musgrove Park Hospital, Taunton. It was while being on 'The District' at Bishops Lydeard that she decided to take the health visitors' course at Oxford and the comprehensive Queen's Nurse training in London, having gained extra experience as a midwife in Taunton. She met Patricia Stowell at Musgrove and they both did the extra courses. Once qualified, the County Nursing Officer suggested they take the 'double district' at Watchet. They lived at 17 South Road in the council property available, rent being deducted from their salaries (for house and furniture). Transport was shared – a Ford car and a bicycle! – until eventually a second car was provided. They covered the geographical area of Blue Anchor, Chapel Cleeve, Old Cleeve, Watchet, Doniford, Liddymore married quarters and West and East Quantoxhead. Their off duty time was one day a week and one weekend a month, and were on call most evenings except before a day off. They had four weeks holiday per year. Equipment was minimal for nursing visits and was carried in two separate bags – one on the carrier, the other in the basket of the bicycle. Syringes were made of glass and forceps, etc., were boiled – no disposables! Terminally ill patients were generally cared for at home, with nursing help and advice; late night morphia injections were sometimes necessary. Dressings were purchased by the patients, most being available on prescription at a charge of 1s. per item, therefore one was very careful with bandages, gauze and cotton wool. These items were sterilized at home by baking in the oven till a light biscuit colour.

As hospital beds were in short supply in the late 1950s and early '60s many babies were born at home, even poor housing did not count. Many houses did not have bathrooms, hot water systems or central heating. One house only had a shared outside tap and the 'loo' was down the garden – a bucket of 'slops' was carried in one hand and a bucket of water in the other! In a caravan no cot was available so Sister Nash went to the local grocer and chose a box from his store – the baby used it until about three months old! Two good-sized bags carried essential equipment, a heavy wooden case housed the gas and air machine, and spare cylinders were carried in a box, Heavy basket scales were used initially, but were later changed for a spring balance type, with baby placed in a net lined with a napkin. The mother was provided with a special pack of dressings for her and the baby, which lasted for a few days, then those prepared by the mother (following instructions). A list of other items needed by the midwife had to be ready four weeks before the baby was due. Soiled dressings were disposed of by burning on an open fire or in a stove; sometimes the local gasworks was approached to burn big bundles as this made it much easier for the families.

Health visiting was mainly done in the afternoons; in the mornings mothers were too busy doing the washing and other household chores. Most houses had coppers for boiling the clothes, some had Baby Birkos for the daily nappy wash; one or two families had a twin-tub washing machine - very few homes had an 'automatic'. Running a house was really hard work, yet many mothers managed to bake cakes and pies in addition to cooking daily wholesome meals, using many vegetables grown in their gardens. Generally babies were weighed at home until six weeks old, then at the child health clinic, where a team of voluntary helpers kept a register, sold baby food, Ovaltine and Marmite. Others made tea for mothers so they could stay and chat, the children being kept occupied with toys on a mill felt kindly provided by Wansbrough Paper Company. From Christmas 1958 a children's party was held, with each child receiving a small present from funds obtained earlier in the year by having a jumble sale. Regular developemental checks were carried out, which ceased when the child was about four years old. Medical examinations and immunisations were given by school medical officers and regular head inspections were made and parents advised when necessary. It was not until the 1960s that vision testing took place. Social life for most mothers in the early 1960s was almost non-existent, and after much thought and encouragement from the Nursing Officers a Mothers' Club was formed. An offer was made to pay rent for a hall for 10 months, providing a programme included topics of a health-related nature. A small committee was formed: Miss K.P Stowell (chairman), Miss V.M. Nash (secretary), Mrs J. Spoor and Mrs J. Willicombe (treasurers). The first meeting was held in the small hut used by the Red Cross, and the speaker was Dr John Lewis. Today the club still meets, is self-suffient and has adapted to meet the needs of members, many of whom are grandmothers. A 40th birthday dinner was held at Knights Templar School, when many former members joined in the celebrations.

In the late 1950s Sister Nash was appointed Nursing Officer for the local Red Cross Detachment. This involved giving home nursing lectures and practical experience to both adult and cadet members. Upon closure of the local branch of the Red Cross the Phoenix Centre, of which she is a trustee, was started and welfare work continued. She was awarded a Badge of Honour and Life Membership for services to the Red Cross. Also in the late 1950s she became a Sunday school teacher (senior girls' class) at the local Methodist Church, later becoming superintendent before retiring in 1987. Sister Nash was persuaded to stand for election to the old Watchet Urban District Council in 1963 and, being successful, served on the Housing Committee and was the Council's representative at the Council School as a Manager and a Governor at Danesfield School.

In 1966 Sister Nash was one of 66 people awarded a Winston Churchill Travelling Fellowship. She wished to find out how Australians managed to provide care in semi-rural/urban towns and how research into toxaemia of pregnancy was progressing, also to look at facilities for senior citizens. As well as visiting Australia, she was able to observe some of the health services in Hong Kong, New Zealand and Fiji and maternity care in San Francisco. It was a wonderful experience and one she will never forget. She was presented with a Churchill Fellows Medallion in 1969 at the Mansion House, London, in recognition of her tour.

Sister Nash resigned from the Urban Council in 1970 when she decided to go to work in Australia for a period. She returned to Watchet to resume her nursing work, and in 1972 the Ugandan Asians were billeted in the old army camp at Doniford. Sister Nash spent almost all her working day there, being involved with helping families to adapt to life in the UK. A team of part-time staff worked in a surgery, but should residents become ill in their quarters she or an assistant would visit to assess the problem, only then would a doctor visit if it was considered necessary. Sister Nash was glad she had worked in a tropical area and knew how to take slides to confirm malaria. Arrivals came in coach-loads and, after passing various sectors, finally reached the medical section. Many women could not speak English, so they had to ask the children to enquire if contraception was being used. One urgent training was found necessary – *how to use an English toilet!* In Uganda it was the practice to squat!

Sister Nash was presented with the Queen's District Nursing Long Service Badge by Princess Anne in 1978. She retired in 1992 and continues to reside in Watchet where she is still involved in a wide range of interests, including representing the local Methodist Church as a Knights Templar School governor; she also enjoys overseas travel.

Well-known Watchet shopkeeper Miss Hibbert chatting in her shop with
world-renowned yachtsman Sir Robin Knox-Johnson and TV producer
Mike Hall whilst they were in the town filming for the programme
Forgotten Ports of the Bristol Channel in 1996. Sir Robin was to visit
Watchet again in 2001 to officially open the Marina. Miss Hibbert ran
her confectionery and bicycle accessory shop in Swain Street for 46 years.
Ellen Myra Hibbert, who was never known by her first name to anyone
but her very closest friends, was forced to close the shop early in 1999
through failing health. A piece of Watchet's history was thus ended, the
old shop being well remembered for its rows of glass jars of sweets, ice
cream, bicycle parts and polite personal service. Miss Hibbert was always
very particular that people said please and thank you, and she became as
much a part of the town as the old-fashioned shop she took over from her
mother, who sold dairy products and game. Miss Hibbert's father had
opened Watchet's first garage behind the Post Office.

Upon leaving school at Taunton, Miss Hibbert qualified as a State
Registered Nurse and mental nurse, ending up working as an industrial
nurse at the Royal Ordnance factory at Puriton. She never wanted
anything to do with the shop, but as years went by she made many friends
there and in the end her shop became quite unique because people could
buy individual bicycle parts rather than having to purchase whole packs of
items.

Miss Hibbert died in December 2001 at the age of 91 years. At the time
of writing, the old shop premises have been converted into Chives Cafe.

Miss Ivy Stephenson holding purses containing the Royal Maundy Money
with which she was presented by the Queen at Wells Cathedral in April,
1993; she had been organist at St Decuman's Church for 57 years and
taught music for over 60 years.

A New Millennium

Work commenced on the construction of Watchet's marina in 2000, being completed the following year. It was opened by renowned yachtsman Sir Robin Knox-Johnson.

A statue of the Ancient Mariner to commemorate Coleridge's famous Rime and his connection with Watchet was erected on the Esplanade by the Watchet Market House Museum Society in 2003.

Watchet Red Cross Centre closed in 2004 and the Phoenix Centre rose in 2005. The old Church School was demolished in 2007 and a housing complex built on the site.

An old local custom was revived on 25th November, 2007 when 'Caturn's Night' was celebrated. It was marked by dancers in period costume, stalls and the consumption of warm apple cake washed down with cider.

The enhancement of the Esplanade was completed in 2008 and in the same year a statue in honour of John Short ('Yankee Jack'), Watchet's famous sailor and shantyman, was erected on the Esplanade by the Watchet Market House Museum Society. It was dedicated to the late Ben Norman, a well-known local personality.

In 2008 it was announced that the parishes of Watchet and Williton were to become a United Benefice with one full-time priest and one part-time.

That year also saw the first music festival organised by the Carnival Club on a separate weekend from the Carnival.

In sport, Watchet Town Football Club won the Somerset Senior Cup in season 2001-2, and won promotion to the Somerset County Premiere League in 2008. Watchet Bowling Club won the Turnbull Cup for the first time in their history in 2005, retaining it in 2006. Watchet 1st XI cricket team won the Herbert Baker Cup Plate in 2006.

Watchet Cricket Club 1st XI, winners of the Herbert Baker Cup Plate, 2006. Playing in the final at Staplegrove against Ilminster, a club from a higher grade, Watchet were the underdogs, but with great team spirit and enthusiastic leadership from Phillip Milton they won in the last over. *Scores:* Ilminster 145-9 (J. Strong 3-43); Watchet 149-7 (J. Harris 39, C. Sully 37, C. Strong 35). *Left to right, back row:* Clive Strong, Chris Wookie, Taylor Maddock, Adam Bishop, Chris Sully, Jason Strong, Norman Yaw; *front:* Philip Sylvester, Ryan Strong, John Harris, David Milton, Martin Strong (coach), Phillip Milton (captain).

Watchet's David Milton stole the show in the town's carnival procession of 2003 with his comic offering of *Oh! What a Beauty*. He won best overall entry, best single walker and most humorous entry. David fully deserved his award, not only for his support of the carnival along with his wife Daphne, but also for all the untiring work and effort he puts in for the benefit of the town.

The Esplanade Club's 2005 Watchet Carnival entry Lilly Marlene. *Left to right, back:* Janet Tapp, Mary Saunders, Rose Jones, Caroline Lee, Alison Robinson, Sally Chamberlain, Helen Chave, Velda Dennis, Dave Wilson; *sitting:* ?, Barbara Ketchen.

Pirates of the Bristol Channel, the Esplanade Club's prize-winning entry in the 2007 Watchet Carnival. *Left to right:* Pat Dennis, Paul Dennis, John Barnes, Velda Dennis, Roy Chave, Roger Sadler, Alison Robinson, Sue Barnes, Barbara Ketchen.

In 2006 Watchet Sea Scouts had their place among the country's elite confirmed following a tough inspection. The group passed with flying colours to remain within the Admiralty Recognition Scheme as one of just 101 Sea Scout groups recognised by the Royal Navy as being the best in the country. The Duke of Edinburgh Bronze Awards were gained by Explorer Scouts Daniel Cooper, Anthony McClelland, Karl Szabo, Tom Anderson and Jacob Daley. Adam Childs and Josh Peters were awarded the Chief Scout's Gold Awards and Karl Szabo the Harold and Hilda Strong Watercraft Shield in recognition of his kayaking and powerboat skills. *Left to right, back row:* Jeremy Szabo, Garth Davis, Tom Anderson, Karl Szabo, Lieutenant Commander John Haynes, Dan Cooper, Anthony McClelland, Kevin Lowe, Watchet Sea Scouts leader Simon Bale, Beverley Wride; *front:* Karl Manley, Josh Peters, Adrian Lowe, Rauri Eastwood, Jacob Daley, Adam Childs.

Watchet Cub Scouts marked the 100th anniversary of the Scouting movement in 2007 with a sunrise celebration in a field above the town at Parsonage Farm. Cubs and leaders renewed their promises in honour of the special centenary year. *Left to right, back row:* Alec Danby (Watchet Town Crier), Amanda Taylor (Assistant Leader), Glenda Bale (Leader), Malcolm Bale (Group Scout Leader), Shirley Harrington (St Decuman's Church reader and a former Assistant District Commissioner), Tom Harrington (former District Commissioner); *middle:* Lawrence Benyon, Jack Groves, Jim Hunt, Liam Hoyle, Declan Patterson, Jaydn Nunn, Regan Kelly-Gallagher, Regan Willicombe, Elliot Morren, Cameron Sandford, Leon Philpott, Henry Mitchell, Sol Pilcher; *front:* Ashley Morby, Liam Morby, Luke Heath, Kelvin Zinyama, Elliot Scott, Nigel Bremner, Stuart Booker, Jack Perkins.

The 1st Watchet Brownies at their 'Winter Wonderland' four-day pack holiday at Crowcombe Hall in 2007. The hall was festooned with Christmas decorations, including a beautifully adorned Christmas tree. During their adventure the Brownies held their own carol service, made Christmas decorations and mince pies, decorated Christmas cakes and even had a full Christmas dinner with all the trimmings. They were visited by Tom and Shirley Harrington, and Shirley helped the Brownies work towards their Stargazer badge. Supervising the Brownies were leaders Katrina Bale, Elisa Day, Mandy Slack and Martha Day. *Left to right, back row:* Megan Trunks, Emma Boustead, Rosie Chamberlain, Mrs Shirley Harrington, Stephanie Bibby, Mr Tom Harrington, Alice Chamberlain, Danniella Garratt; *middle:* Bethany Sherrin, Emily Champion, Niamh Garbut, Leah Mann, Coral Osman, Harriet Marshall; *front:* Helen Sun, Sophie Aspey, Dayna Walsh, Natasha Fisher, Alicia Beck, Tamsin Ferguson.

Members of Watchet Phoenix Centre on the London Eye, 2004. *Left to right:* Grace Brown, Jack Binding, Malcolm Brown, Joyce Bacon, Lilian Downer, Daphne Barrass, Phyllis Pugsley, Dilys Bryant, Pat Berry; *sitting:* Mavis Bryant, David ('Toby') Bryant.

A group of ladies from Watchet who joined with a team of 52 from Minehead and Williton to travel to London to take part in the Playtex Moonwalk of 2005. This is an annual event to raise money for breast cancer and cancer care research, and involves walking a marathon 26.2 miles during the night. The West Somerset group raised a staggering £18,000 and all members of the Watchet contingent completed the course. *Left to right, back:* Barbara Cornish, Laine Stevens, Emily Hawes, Linda Redd, Gill Bishop, Shelley Goodwill, Karen Woodfield, Heather Crockford, Sally Stewart, Glenda Maddock, Sue Wood, Suzette Jones, Emma Sully, Julie Sully, Christine Waterman; *lady in middle:* ?; *front:* Nicola Mossman, Teresa Arthington, Diane Allen, Sandra Holness. Other Watchet walkers not pictured were Joanne Knight, Linda Bulpin and Marilyn Binding.

New Year Millennium party at Knights Templar School, 2000. *Among those pictured are:* David Milton, Bernadette Wheeler, Dave Wheeler, Robin Saddington, Graham White, Ray Tew, Mr Pople, Chris Waterman, Jack White, Ben Saddington, Ben Waterman, Nick Jones, Craig Owen, Emma Jones, Julie Sully, Pete Owen, Debbie Owen, Rob Jones, Suzette Jones, Andrew Wheeler, Stella Alexander, Caron Pople, Mrs Pople, Steve Waterman, Stuart Pople, Jess Pople, Debbie Saddington, Jess Saddington, Pat Tew, Joe Bolton, Julie Bolton, Kate Bolton, Myles Jones, Mark Bolton, Daphne Milton, Josh Moore, Ollie Saddington, Jackie White, Kate White, Lee Owen, Emma Sully, Chris Sully, Ollie Waterman, Chris Pople, Matthew Wheeler, Phillip Milton.

'Fail Not At Your Peril'

It is quite possible that the origin of Watchet Court Leet goes back a thousand years, for Watchet was a 'defended town' in the 10th century and the site of a Royal Mint. For hundreds of years until about 1830 all matters of importance to the town were dealt with by the recognised authority – the Court Leet. Every year in October a number of well-known men of the town were summoned to attend the Court at the Bell Inn in Market Street 'at Twelve o'clock in the forenoon precisely' and warned by the Bailiff to 'Fail not at your peril'.

All sessions of the Court were presided over by the Steward of Wyndham Estate – delegated by the Lord of the Manor. Each man, after being 'sworn in', was appointed as an official of the Court and, whether he liked it or not, had to take on certain duties for a year's duration. The appointments were as follows: Port Reeve (to collect ground rents, tolls and certain harbour cargo dues), Inspector of Weights and Measures, Inspector of Nuisances, Ale Taster, two Stock Drivers (to impound straying animals), Foreman of the Jury, Recorder, Town Crier, two Constables and two Scavengers. In addition, all had to serve on the jury whenever wrongdoers were brought before the Court.

At the annual meeting in October, after the obligatory swearing in and the appointment of each officer in turn, everyone sat down to enjoy a traditional dinner of roast goose, followed by apple pie and cream, then walnuts. A noggin of a secret recipe hot punch was then ladled out and glasses raised to toast the reigning monarch, then again to the Lord of the Manor. Thus it was that each year countless generations of Watchet men were pressed into service to ensure law and order and the smooth running of the town. Gradually, from about 1830, regional police authorities and county councils took over the functions of the many Courts Leet throughout the country. Most of them, therefore,

disbanded or just faded away. Fortunately this did not happen at Watchet where local people, and in particular the Wyndham family, recognised the Court Leet to be a colourful link with the past.

Watchet's Court Leet, therefore, never disbanded and in October each year, after receiving the usual

Watchet Court Leet, 2005. *Left to right, back row:* T. Knight, D. Binding, N. Swinburne, B. Norman, G. Coggins, H Llewellyn (Court President), R. White, R. Dibble, R. Burnell; *front:* J. Binding (Bailiff), D. Quint, N. Tapp, P.J. Addicott (guest speaker), M. Bale, M. Parsons, R. Wedlake, A. Danby (Town Crier).

warning from the bailiff, men still assemble at the Bell Inn. Here, as in the past, after swearing allegiance etc., each man is delighted to be appointed to one of the traditional duties.

With the ceremony over they all sit down to enjoy the long-established roast goose dinner, etc., as well as their noggin of hot punch. Today, apart from the bailiff, who still issues his threatening summons in October, the only officer to actually carry out his duties is the Town Crier. Whenever called upon, he will don his colourful regalia and attract attention by ringing his bell and loudly announcing any forthcoming events. Although it is very unlikely ever to be called upon to administer justice, Watchet Court Leet still maintains its old lock-up jail in Market Street – just in case!

The gratifying sum of £950 was raised at a coffee and mince pie morning held at the home of Tony Knight in December, 2006. Organised by Tony and the local Conservative branch committee, it was also supported by local organisations and residents for the funds of Children's Hospice South-West. The event continued a tradition that has been running for over 30 years for various charities. *Left to right:* Kirsty Cornish, Tony Knight (holding grand-daughter Mollie-May Cornish), Valerie Norman, MBE, Pam Thomas; *holding cheque:* June Daley.

Watchet Women's Section of the Royal British Legion celebrated their 75th birthday with a special anniversary tea at the Clubhouse in 2006. *Left to right, back row:* Kath Edwards, Muriel Seabrook, Joan Allen, Mr Allen, Unice ?, Wendy Richards, Lilian Harrod, Mr Sparkes, Debbie Russell, Barry Barrall (chairman, Watchet Men's Section), Muriel Bryant, Teresa Potter (chairman), Molly Clinton (secretary); *sitting:* Audrey Burke, Piper Heal, Joan Webb (assistant county secretary), Kath Sparkes (county secretary), Pam Whitehead (national ceremonial officer), Georgina Pope.

Some of the hard-working members of Watchet Carnival Club, 2006. *Left to right, back row:* Gerry Lowe, Nigel Pike, Cedric Lewis, Robert Hornby, Kevin Prescott; *front:* Jackie Bale, Mark Bale (club chairman), Lorraine Binding. At the time of writing, the above were also involved in the organisation of a superb three-day music festival at Parsonage Farm, which culminated with a Sunday night prom followed by a brilliant fireworks display. This festival in 2008 was the first to be held on different dates to the carnival weekend and attracted large crowds.

Well-known Watchet Morris dancer Dudley Binding, c.2000.

Watchet WI celebrate the Queen's Golden Jubilee in 2002. *Left to right, back:* Jackie Stanton, Ann Binding, Peggy Wheel, Doreen Morse, Ethel Kirby, Joyce Dunn, Peggy Norton, Betty Madge, Shirley Williams, Jenny Hill, June Roberts, Hannah Branfield, Ray Hudson, Janet Martin, Patricia Baynham; *front:* Diana Bale, Vera Garrard, Jean Date, Maidie Ford, Jessie Norman.

Watchet golfer Warren Knight became one of Minehead and West Somerset Golf Club's youngest-ever champions at the age of 17 in 2008. He recorded a winning double by having both the best nett and gross scores in the club championship. In the same year Warren was also the club's junior open champion and winner of the Minehead and West Somerset junior championship. Warren is pictured holding his trophies.

Watchet Red Cross colour party at the Remembrance Sunday parade, 2007. *Left to right:* Peter Darrell, Eddie May, Bernice Danby, Nigel Swinburne, David Bryant.

Watchet and District Choral Society, 2008. *Left to right, back row:* John Parsons, Donald Butterworth (secretary), David Ridley (chairman), Geoff Dennett, Alan Jones, David Hait, John Ward (accompanist's assistant), Elizabeth Manning (accompanist); *fourth row:* Iorworth Jones, Rodney Ettery (treasurer), Michael Freeman, Alan Fisher, Alan Marler, Margaret Pye, Janet Strong: *third row:* June Hanna, Ann Dobson, Julie Partington, Mary Rhodes, Jacqueline Butterworth, Elizabeth Steadman, Sharron Costley; *second row:* Pam Freeman, Janet Dixon, Jean Cheetham, Valerie Cossor, Sarah Griffiths, Janet Lee, Ellie Jones, Mary Parsons, Valerie Ward, Ethel Kirby; *front:* Jacilyn Binding, Dorothy Lee, Maureen Oldfield, Gay Chilcott, Patricia Abbott (conductor), Shirley Dee, Iris Williams, Mary Slade, Mary Copp.

Remembrance Day at Watchet, 2002. *Left to right:* Ben Norman, Jack Binding, Malcolm Brown, Howard Strong.

The commitment of historian Ben Norman, a founder-member of Watchet Market House Museum, was honoured in 2005 with a special presentation. To mark Ben's retirement after 15 years as curator, he was presented by fellow members of the Museum Society with a maquette of the Ancient Mariner, a prototype of the impressive statue designed by Alan Herriot that now graces Watchet's Esplanade. After his retirement as curator, Ben became consultant to his successor, Roger Wedlake, son of the first curator. *Pictured left to right are:* Roger Wedlake, Ben Norman, Malcolm Brown (founder-member and chairman).

After retirement from English Heritage and the Monument Commission, Watchet resident Bob Reed decided, among other things, to take up making and carving walking sticks as a hobby. His ambition was to make a different stick for every day of the year. Bob is pictured in 2006 with well over 200 of his sticks.

Formed in 2002, Watchet Sea Rowing Club christened its new boat *Sarah Pilkington* in 2006. It is the first ever Celtic longboat to be fitted with sliding seats, and was named after the last rowed lifeboat to operate from Watchet harbour. The ceremony was performed by one of its former crew, Ben Norman. In June of 2006 club members rowed the *Sarah Pilkington* from Barry to Watchet in four hours and eight minutes, having to combat lumpy seas and strong winds for two-thirds of the crossing. *Left to right:* Town crier Alec Danby, Ben Norman, Bob Hornby.

Members of Watchet Sea Rowing Club after the christening of the club's new boat, *Sarah Pilkington*, in 2006. The boat was given a traditional Celtic blessing by the Vicar of St Decuman's, the Revd David Ireson. *Left to right:* Geraldine Hollweg, Tony James (chairman), Jude Johnson-Smith, Jayne Yianni, Lesley Abbott-Garner (club captain), Sue Onley, Revd David Ireson, Tara Jones, Matt Jones (behind Tara, men's captain), George Stewart, Liz Stewart (youth development officer), David Hollier, Leigh Parker, Laura Danby (ladies' captain), Bob Hornby, Ken Allen, Johnny Abbott-Garner.

Four sages of Watchet, 2006. *Left to right:* Ken Holness, Geoff Watts, Tony ('Jacker') Sully, Les Reeder.

Watchet Market House Museum steward Derek Hawkins receiving musical greetings from piper Fred Bacon on his 80th birthday, 2007. Vocal greetings were rendered by town crier Alec Danby.

John Nash about to launch the new-style flatner boat in Watchet Marina, 2007.

Watchet Boat Museum launched a new-style of flatner boat in 2007 and named the class after John Short, Watchet's most famous sailor and shantyman, known as 'Yankee Jack'. The new class is called 'The Short Flatner'. Flatners, known as flatties at Watchet, were a very unusual type of fishing boat, almost flat-bottomed with a sharply pointed overhanging bow and stern. This type of boat was not used for sea-fishing anywhere around the coast of Britain except from Watchet and the River Parrett at Bridgwater.

The new flatner reunites with the past in that it is designed using features found on traditional flatners. It was built single-handedly in the museum by curator John Nash and designed in consultation with Commander G.I. Mayes, the museum's president. The 12ft 8in boat is suitable for calm waters and can take three people on board.

A larger Watchet flattie, aptly named *Yankee Jack* after sailor John Short, was built in 1997 by local writer Tony James, who later sailed it around the entire South West peninsular. This recreated the voyages made by Short in the 1890s when he was mate of the Watchet-owned ketch *Annie Christian*. This prompted Tony to chart the experience in a resulting book, *Yankee Jack Sails Again*.

Well-known Watchet farmer Richard Burnell, of Parsonage Farm. He is the third generation of Burnells to farm Parsonage.

Alan Woollam ended a link with school-children in Watchet stretching back 37 years when he retired as headteacher from Knights Templar First School in 2007. He took over the reins of the former St Decuman's School at the age of 25, becoming Somerset's youngest head. This school was his first teaching post after leaving college in 1970 and he simply never left, dedicating his entire career to educating Watchet youngsters.

Alan had only been teaching for four years when he was appointed head, having served one year as deputy head. Fourteen years later he was given the top job of the amalgamated St Decuman's and Watchet County First School to steer architects through the construction of a new purpose-built complex, which became the completed Knights Templar CE and Methodist Community VA First School in 1990. One of the highspots of Alan's career came in 2002 when he was named as the best headteacher of the year in the South West in a national award scheme.

Alan was the recipient of many gifts of appreciation of his dedicated work for the town at farewell gatherings, also a hoard of chocolate and other presents from pupils. His main sporting love is rugby, having played for Minehead Barbarians and Bridgwater and Albion clubs. Alan resides at Williton with his wife Melanie, who also retired from teaching in 2007.

A permanent reminder of his link with Watchet has been given to Alan with the naming of the housing complex on the site of the former St Decuman's School in South Road as Woollams Place in his honour.

Well-known Watchet builder John Stone plying his skill as a stonemason at the top of Goviers Lane, 2008.

Watchet lost one of its most fervent and well-known sons in January, 2008 with the death of W.H. (Ben) Norman. Born in Gladstone Terrace on Christmas Day, 1918, he was named William Henry - his father's choice after one of the family's ships as they were a maritime family - but his mother wanted him called Ben, a name by which he was always known. By coincidence, Ben's mother was also born on a Christmas Day.

Ben attended the local Council school and upon leaving learnt his trade as plumber, painter and decorator. As a boy he used to sail with his father across to the Welsh coast and to Appledore with Captain Reuben Chichester on the ketches *Bonita* and *Democrat*. Apart from five years of Army service during the Second World War, Ben lived in the town he loved all his life. Its history, particularly Watchet's maritime connections, remained an abiding passion. Ben was the longest serving member of Watchet Court Leet, 2008 being his 50th year; he was also proud to have been a member of Watchet Hobblers' Association. For a period he served as a member of Watchet Urban District Council. Another activity with which Ben will be well remembered was the summer trips he ran on his boat the *Lyn* from Watchet harbour to Blue Anchor Bay. These were enjoyed by countless visitors and locals alike.

Ben was a founder-member and for 15 years curator of Watchet Market House Museum. His enthusiasm for the museum was unbounding, working tirelessly and putting countless hours into its development. Ben was one of the prime instigators in the Market House Museum Society's project in erecting the statue of the Ancient Mariner (from Coleridge's renowned Rime) on the Esplanade in 2003. His last major ambition was to see John Short ('Yankee Jack'), Watchet's famous sailor and shantyman, duly honoured with the erection of an appropriate statue on the Esplanade. Ben strove hard to bring this to fruition and a statue was commissioned by the Market House Museum Society, but sadly he was not to see his ambition fulfilled. However, the statue was erected in March 2008, and was appropriately unveiled by his widow Margaret. The statue is dedicated to Ben for all his endeavour in securing its erection. A story board giving details of John Short's life, written by Ben, stands adjacent to the statue.

The author of several books, Ben's most successful is probably his definitive *Tales of Watchet Harbour*, which has run into three editions. Others include *Legends and Folklore of Watchet* and *Minehead, Dunster and Watchet in Old Prints*. His last literary venture was with the authors of this book who had the privilege of working with him in producing *The Book of Watchet and Williton Revisited*.

For relaxation Ben was never happier than reeling off sea shanties and folk tunes on his melodion and he readily played at social gatherings and entertained the elderly.

Ben is survived by his wife Margaret, whom he married in 1954, daughter Linda, sons Barry and Daniel, and grandchildren Ruby, Jack, Sally and Arielle.

Well-known Watchet postman Michael ('Zippy') Shopland, 2007. 'Zippy' has been delivering mail in Watchet for 23 years.

Local postman Darren Scott with a Royal Mail delivery hand trolley on its first day out at Watchet on 26th January 2008. Darren has completed 10 years service as a postman.

Born in Nantymoel, South Wales, of Watchet parents in 1923, Jack Binding came to Watchet at the age of four years. He was educated at St Decuman's Church School and The Halletts Commercial College, Taunton. In 1939 he was employed by Risdon & Co in the Food Control Office at Williton, transferring to local government in 1950 as finance officer for Williton Rural District and Watchet Urban District Councils; he later became chief financial officer to both authorities. He was involved in post-war major schemes such as Hinkley Point power station, coast protection and bringing water supplies and sewerage to rural villages. With the formation of West Somerset District Council in 1974, Jack was appointed the new authority's internal auditor. He took early retirement in 1982.

Keenly interested in sport, Jack played cricket for Watchet for many years, and was also involved in local tennis and badminton. He was also a supporter of Watchet Football Club, serving on its committee for a period. A lifelong Methodist, Jack is still active in the community, being a member and, at the time of writing, chairman of Watchet Market House Museum Society, a member of Watchet Phoenix, and takes a keen interest in the West Somerset Railway and local affairs.

Jenny Hill (neé Hunt) was born in Watchet, being a member of a well-known local family. She resided there for the first 22 years of her life until her marriage, after which she left the town for 30 years, travelling extensively with her husband during his Army service. On her return to Watchet with her husband in 1991 she was employed with the NHS based at Williton, being personal assistant to the manager of the community nurses. Following retirement, being already a member of Watchet Town Council, she decided to seek election to West Somerset District Council. After successfully being elected and re-elected as one of the Watchet district councillors, she has served on the authority for nine years, being chairman and vice-chairman of various committees. Jenny was elected chairman of the District Council for 2007-8.

Arthur Pye was born and brought up in Rochdale, Lancashire, where he met his wife Irene. With his family, he came to Watchet in 1948 to take up the post of sub-postmaster, a position he remained in until his retirement in 1988. Another reason for coming to Watchet was to be near his wife's mother, who was the eldest daughter of John and Elizabeth Hunt, of Alexandra Villas.

Shortly after arriving at Watchet, Arthur joined the Watchet and District Choral Society and sang with them for approximately 30 years. A keen supporter of Watchet Town Football Club, he served on its committee for a period. Another of Arthur's interests is the Watchet Town Band, of which he is a vice-president and was a playing member for over 30 years. He taught his elder daughter and two grand-daughters to play musical instruments in the band. A lifelong member of the Methodist Church, Arthur has sung in the local church choir, been a Sunday school teacher and held many offices within the church.

Mrs Margaret Norman after unveiling the fine statue on the Esplanade to honour John Short ('Yankee Jack'), Watchet's famous sailor and shantyman, on a bitterly cold Easter Saturday, 22 March, 2008. Gesturing towards the statue is its sculptor, Alan Herriot, of Penicuik, Scotland. The project was the idea of Margaret's late husband Ben Norman, a lifelong Watchet townsman, a former curator of the Market House Museum and local author. Sadly, he did not live to see his project come to fruition. However, the statue was commissioned by the Watchet Market House Museum Society and, fittingly, was unveiled by his widow. The statue is dedicated to Ben and this is recorded on a plaque at its base. A storyboard giving details of John Short's life, written by Ben, stands adjacent to the statue. The ceremony was attended by descendants of John Short, officers and committee of the Market House Museum Society, local dignitaries and many townsfolk. The Watchet Town Band was in attendance and sea shanties were played and sung by George Ody and his group. The master of ceremonies was Town Crier Alec Danby.

John Short sailed the world in a range of sailing ships as an able seaman and later as a bosun. In the 1860s some of his ships ran the blockade in the American Civil War and it was because of this that he was awarded the nickname of 'Yankee Jack'. It was a tradition aboard larger sailing ships for the crew to sing sea shanties and John Short's strong and tuneful voice often led him to take a solo role. Over the years he memorised the words and tunes of dozens of shanties and had many of the melodies from his repertoire transcribed by two eminent collectors of folk songs and shanties, Cecil Sharp and Sir Richard Terry. John Short died in 1933 at the great age of 94 and was buried in St Decuman's churchyard.

Grouped around the statue of John Short ('Yankee Jack') after its unveiling in 2008 are, *left to right:* Town Crier Alec Danby, Mrs Margaret Norman, Alan Herriot (sculptor of the statue), Jack Binding (chairman, Watchet Market House Museum Society).

A young Vernon Stone aboard the Royal Mail Line's passenger ship *Aragon* in Santos, Brazil. Vernon left Watchet Church School, where he was the first head boy, at the age of 15 to attend the British Sailors' Society Prince of Wales Sea Training School at Dover. He was the last known born and bred Watchet boy to sail out of Watchet on a British flagged ship, *Kyle of Lochalsh*, which brought esparto grass from Algeria to Watchet for the paper mills at Silverton. At the time of writing, Vernon is employed by West Somerset Council in the positions of harbourmaster at Watchet and Minehead.

Watchet Town Crier Alec Danby cutting the ribbon to mark the official opening of the enhancement of the town's Esplanade in April 2008. Civic leaders, dignitaries and local people turned out in force to watch the ceremony and then enjoy a day of activities and fun. Alec is watched by, *from the left:* Cllr David Banks (Watchet Town Council chairman), Cllr Jenny Hill (West Somerset Council chairman and Watchet Town councillor) and Cllr Keith Ross (West Somerset Council leader).

Presentation of a wooden plaque by Watchet Town Council chairman Cllr David Banks to Alec Danby to commemorate his 21 years as town crier. Civic leaders used the official opening of Watchet's revamped Esplanade in 2008 as a backdrop for the presentation. Alec, a former regular soldier, regimental sergeant major and retired postman, has travelled the world in his town crier capacity and has represented Watchet on home ground on thousands of occasions as well as winning the Town Criers' Guild championship in 1990. Being Watchet's first uniformed town crier, Alec is now on his third costume.

In 2001 Andrew Woodward became the first boxer from Watchet to represent his country. He was one of just six boxers to be selected for the England Under-19s squad against Young Scotland in London. Andrew, a light-welterweight, won his bout against a seven-times Scottish national champion. He went on to represent and captain the England amateur boxing squad in further international tournaments.

Andrew began boxing at the age of eight with Watchet Amateur Boxing Club, thus following a family tradition as he is a nephew of the Jones family of boxers. He progressed over the years to be the England Youth Amateur Boxing Association light-welterweight champion as well as achieving several other amateur boxing honours.

Educated at Knights Templar School, Danesfield School and West Somerset College, Andrew was among just 24 talented teenagers from across Britain to attend boxing's first residential Academy of Excellence at East Durham and Houghall College.

Andrew has now retired from boxing and plies his trade as a plumber around the world, having travelled extensively. A gifted sportsman, he is also keen on soccer and cricket and has played for Watchet and Minehead first teams at the latter.

Esplanade Club Pool Team, 2002-3. *Left to right:* Paul Walters, Steve Groves, Albert Foster, Paddy Gower, Bob Izzard, Steve Ashby, Dennis Smith.

The Has Beens skittles team, 2001. *Left to right, back row:* Richard Binding, Chris Milton, Colin Norman, Tim Milton (sticker-up); *front:* Eddie Chapman, Roy Williams, Cliff Milton, Dennis Allen.

Watchet and District Skittles League team Jack, 2005. *Left to right, back:* R. Milton, S. Wood, B. Harding, S. Bosley, R. Middleton, C. Brown; *front:* A. Pyne.

Some of the former players who attended Watchet Town Football Club's reunion in 2007. *Left to right:* Nick Sully, Derek Chidgey, Steve Allen, ?, Ralph Allen, Chris Milton, Dennis Williams, Dave Sully, Alfie Edwards, ?, Jimmy Martin, Pat West, Harry Husband, Trevor Webber, John Spoor, Malcolm Bale, Ron Bryan, Colin Norman, Tony West, ?, Brian Redd, Mervyn Parsons, Bert Bothwick.

The Watchet Town FC squad who won promotion to the Somerset County Premiere League in 2008. *Left to right, back row:* Mike Stout, Steve Wild, Gary Trunks, John Harris, Adam Bishop, Matt Heywood, Chris Sully, Matt Knowles, Jamie Milton; *front:* Nick Sully (manager), Lawrence Monaghan, Louis Allen, Dominic Richards, Simon Chilcott, Jason Worth, Paul Raymond, Matt Cox.

Born and bred in Watchet, Mervyn Parsons has been involved in many different sporting activities in his lifetime and still umpires five or six times a week at cricket matches all over the county and further afield. Aged 80 and still residing in the town at the time of writing, Mervyn began his involvement with cricket through scoring for the local team, which at that time included Wally Rawle, Edward Martin, Nick Sully, Andy Milton, Bill Strong, Raymond Clavey, Ron Rendell, Michael ('Buster') Jones, David Bendle, Donald Binding, Douglas Webber and Roger Suchley among others. Mervyn admits he was never a brilliant player and started umpiring when no-one else wanted to go out in the middle, so he picked up the white coat. Following that he went on the umpires' panel for the Somerset League, where he has served for 37 years. He says he loves umpiring and gets a great deal of pleasure from being involved with the game. Mervyn has umpired hundreds of games, during which he has seen thousands of players, some of whom have gone on to higher things. He came across former England captain Nasser Hussain when he was taking part as a young lad in the King's College festival at Taunton. Mervyn has umpired at that festival since its inception.

Soccer was also a big attraction to Mervyn, playing for Watchet Casuals as a youngster. This side was run by well-known Watchet character 'Crickey' Chidgey. During his service with the RAF just after the Second World War, Mervyn started to referee football matches, going on to officiate many games in the Western League, where he became a well-known official on the second division circuit. Continuing officiating for 34 years, Mervyn said the most important game he ever refereed was an FA Cup derby between Bideford and Barnstaple. His command performance as a referee was when Princess Margaret was visiting Butlin's at Minehead in the 1960s and Mervyn was chosen to take charge of a youth soccer match staged for her benefit. He was also involved with the Watchet Amateur Boxing Club and was on the South-West Boxing Panel, helping out in various capacities at tournaments. For 35 years Mervyn has given yeoman service to the Watchet and District Skittles League as secretary and treasurer.

Away from sport, Mervyn is a jazz enthusiast, regularly travelling to London to visit Ronnie Scott's club; he is also a member of Watchet Court Leet, the Watchet Market House Museum Society and the Rotary Club of the Quantocks. In his younger days he was an accomplished exponent on the dance floor, winning six gold medals for ballroom dancing. Mervyn spent all his working life as an accountant at the Wansbrough Paper Mill.

Watchet Cricket Club, Somerset League Division 3 winners, 2005. *Left to right, back row:* Raymond Clavey (president), Rod Richards, Clive Strong, Liam Woolgrove, Philip Sylvester, Norman Yaw, Matt Lovell, Doug Webber (umpire), Ivor Lovell; *front:* Andy Pyne, Jason Strong, Martin Strong (captain), Chris Sully, John Harris.

Watchet Cricket Club Under 13s in an inter-club match, 2006. *Left to right, back row:* Dean Manley, Aaron Nunn, Edward Jeromson, Joshua Parker, David Milton (youth coach), Ryan Dellow, Sam Nunn, Matthew Danby, Connor Jeromson, Harriet Coleman; *front:* Harry Duncan, Ian Lowe, Mark Bishop, Sam Broadey, Charles Gay, Ryan Jones, Steven Thompson; *on ground:* Daniel Darrell, Matthew Burge.

Dramatic pictures of huge waves lashing the west pier of Watchet harbour, 12 March 2008.

Enhancement of Watchet Esplanade in 2008 with new seating, paving slabs, trees, shrubs and the renovation of the shelters.

Aerial view of Watchet marina and outer harbour, 2008.

Subscribers

Les and Gill Allen, Williton

John and Jean Andow, Cannonville, Sundays River,
  South Africa

Joyce Bacon, Watchet

Glenda and Malcolm Bale, Watchet

John M. Barnes, Watchet, Somerset

Mrs Pat Berry, formally of Watchet

S. D. and M. W. Binding, Watchet

Jack and Jackie Binding, Watchet

Malcolm and Grace Brown, Watchet, Somerset

David and Dilys Bryant, Watchet, Somerset

K. J. Burrow, Bucks Cross, Devon

Mr and Mrs Mark Champion, Watchet, Somerset

Mike and Wendy Chapman, Yeovil, Somerset

Roy and Helen Chave, Watchet, Somerset

Kevin and Elizabeth Chidgey, Penrith, NSW, Australia

Desmond Kenneth Chidgey, Cardiff

Maurice and Joyce Chidgey (née Chave), Watchet,
  Somerset

Gay Chilcott, Watchet

Sheila and Angela Chubb, Watchet

Felicity Clarke, Minehead, Somerset

Diane Clausen

John Coggins, Clevedon

Dorothy M. Coles, South Molton, Devon

Chris Cooke, Watchet, Somerset

Dorothy Cooke, Watchet, Somerset

Peter and Barbara Cornish, Watchet

Dean, Kirsty (née Knight) and Mollie-May Cornish,

Roy and Theresa Date, Watchet, Somerset

Annette Dickinson (née Chidgey), Samuel Dickinson
  & Lee Graham, Exeter, Devon

Lilian F. Stevens Downer

Joan Edwards

Tony and Ruth Everett (née Norman), Watchet

Mrs C. A. Fiddes (née Reeder), Bourne, Lincs

Anita and Kally Finch, Watchet, Somerset

Liz Hamshere, Watchet

Jenny Hill, Watchet, Somerset

Kenneth E. Holness

Dawn Hornby, Watchet

The House family, formerly of Almyr Terrace

David G. Howe, Thatcham, Berks

Jean Howe, Watchet, Somerset

Bryan J. Howe, Minehead, Somerset

Craig, Linda and Bradley Howells, Watchet

Gowan Hunt

Dr Julian B. Hunt, Virginia Water, Surrey

Violet M. James, Watchet

Joan G. Jones, Watchet, Somerset

Robert and Suzette Jones, Watchet, Somerset

Dulcie D. Joslin, Watchet, Somerset

Stephen R. Joslin, Redcar, Yorkshire

Tony Knight, Watchet

Judy Kyte (née McMillan), Watchet and Taunton

Peggy Leach, Bradford-on-Avon

Michael Leat, Bristol

John Lee, Shepton Mallet, Somerset

Jean Lewis, Watchet, Somerset

Ann M. Lewis

Michael A. Lewis, Watchet, Somerset

Christopher Marshall, Watchet, Somerset

Stuart McMillan, Watchet and Penarth

Mr and Mrs David Milton, Watchet, Somerset

Virginia (Ginny) Nash

James, Michelle and Hanna Nicholas, Watchet,
  Somerset

Spike and Kate (née Knight) Norman

David Norton, Watchet

Tommy Perkins, Watchet, Somerset

Margaret Perring (née Reed), Watchet

Stephen, Lisa, Ethan and Ebony Plenty (née Chidgey), Alcombe, Minehead

E. Basil Poole, Aldridge, West Midlands

Jennie Priscott (née Stronach), Bath and Watchet

W.T.J. Rawle, Watchet, Somerset

Les Reeder, Watchet, Somerset

Frank and Val Richards, Doniford

Sheila and Ray Rigglesford, London

Elizabeth Roberts, Watchet, Somerset

Anne Roberts, Watchet

Ken and June Roberts (née Stone), Watchet, Somerset

Mrs J. Sadler (née Perkins), Watchet, Somerset

Elva Seldon (née Willicombe), Bridgwater

Sheila Sherrin, Carhampton

Roy Shopland, Ottery St Mary

Sue Simon and Catherine Upstone, Watchet, Somerset

Christine Somerfield, Watchet, Somerset

Martin Stevens, Watchet

Mr Harry Stiling, Watchet

Gladys Stone, South Yardley, Birmingham

Mr William F.H. Stone, East Quantoxhead

Mr and Mrs W.G. Strong, Watchet, Somerset

David William Sully MBE

Martin R. Sutton, Arundel, West Sussex

Diana Tipper (née McMillan), Watchet and Taunton

Nathan, Ginnette, Alex, Ben and Fern Towells, Watchet

Joy and Keith Towells, Watchet

Christine, Ron and William Turner, Watchet, Somerset

Christine and Steve Waterman, Watchet

Mike Webber, Watchet, Somerset

T. Webster, Watchet, Somerset

Patrick H. West, Taunton

Loretta and Michael Whetlor, Watchet

Peter M. White, Honiton, Devon

Richard Whittington, Bath

Mrs Sue Williams, Bridgwater

Alan George Woollam,

Mrs Audrey Young (née Haines), Colinbrook, Slough, Berks